Dedication

To my family - present and future.

Acknowledgements

Now that "This Doctor's Journey" is finished it hardly seems possible that I needed so much prodding to start it. How could I have put off what turned out to be such a rewarding experience? So to all who listened to my stories and tales over the years and urged me to write a book, I say thank you. If you enjoy reading it you can thank my wife, Doris, who was so insistent that I get on with it.

I also thank Betty Annand who, from her experience at writing a book, gave me wise counsel, and to Doris and my niece, Leslie Franklin, who were able to decipher my terrible writing and transform it into a legible format. And finally to Ann Kask, for her patience with me and her great help in getting this published, I say thank you.

Contents

1	My Roots	9
2	The Journey Begins	20
3	Off to School	31
4	Leaving Home	40
5	College Days	47
6	Montreal and McGill	57
7	Medical School	68
8	Internship	80
9	Kootenay Country	88
10	The Royal City	100
11	Back Home	117
12	Municipal Affairs	124
13	Reflections	132

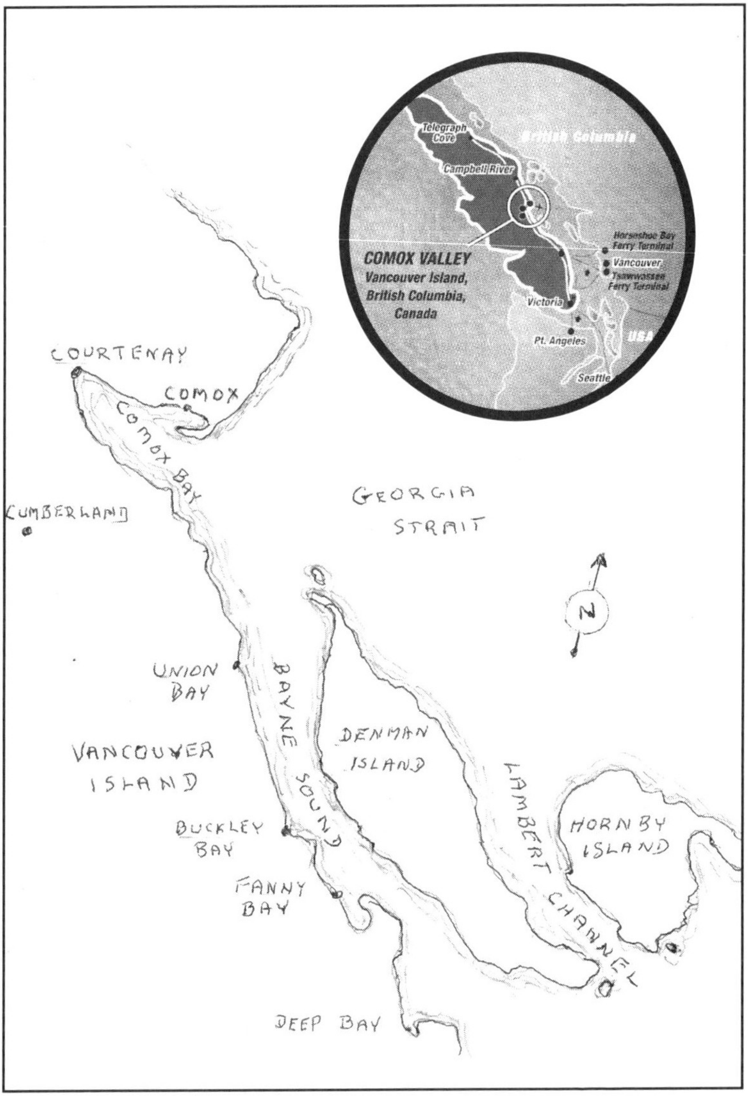
Telegraph Cove
British Columbia
Campbell River
Horseshoe Bay Ferry Terminal
COMOX VALLEY
Vancouver Island, British Columbia, Canada
Vancouver
Tsawwassen Ferry Terminal
Victoria
Pt. Angeles
USA
Seattle
COURTENAY
COMOX
COMOX BAY
CUMBERLAND
GEORGIA STRAIT
N
UNION BAY
BAYNE SOUND
DENMAN ISLAND
VANCOUVER ISLAND
LAMBERT CHANNEL
HORNBY ISLAND
BUCKLEY BAY
FANNY BAY
DEEP BAY

To Commemorate the 100th anniversary of the arrival of the Piercy Family in the Comox Valley

Unveiled by His Honour Walter S. Owen Lieutenant Governor of British Columbia July 7, 1974

Irvine Piercy and Celena Ballson

Chapter I

My Roots

On August 23, 1923 the marriage of Celena Agnes Ballson to Mr. Edward Irvine Piercy of Denman Island took place in Holy Trinity Church, Vancouver, B.C.

Weddings in August are not that uncommon. However this one, where Irvine and Celena were united in Holy Matrimony was of great significance and importance to me. The participants were to become my parents - saddled with the task of raising me. I'm told that at times that was not an easy task.

Just who were these people that had such a diverse educational background? They were of a different religious faith. One was born and grew up in a bustling city, the other in a semi isolated rural setting. There was an age difference of fourteen years. How did they have such an influence on my development and on my future? How did they play such a role in promoting their ethical and moral values which they hoped I would emulate? Why did they place such a high priority on family happiness and respect and pride in one's heritage? All of this would come to me in later years as I learned more and more about them. For now they were just Mother and Dad. To all others in the community they were Celena and Irvine.

My Mother, Celena, was the youngest child of Herbert George Ballson and Sophia Morehouse Fowler. Herbert was born and raised in the town of Rampisham in Dorset, England. After attending public school he apprenticed as a wheelwright. At the age of nineteen he had the desire for adventure and to get involved in the quest for gold that was happening all over the West Coast. So he left his parents, a brother and four sisters and emigrated to America.

Years later, on a trip to Southern England, I visited this area of Dorset and found it to be a very attractive and desirable and prosperous part of the country. I often wonder what impulses a person must have to give up a very secure existence to begin a new life in a new, strange and underdeveloped part of the world. This lust for adventure was not passed on to me in my genes.

He spent the next couple of years in California before moving to Victoria, B.C. where he worked as a carpenter. After two years here he again moved to Burrard Inlet arriving in 1869. He acquired property in what was known as Gastown. After a short stint in the Cassiar region of B.C. as a prospector he returned to the coast where he was to remain for the rest of his life.

As an early settler in this unorganized area he became very interested and involved in the process of acquiring municipal status for the area. This part of the world was about to experience rapid growth because of the final extension of the Canadian Pacific Railroad from Port Moody to Burrard Inlet. Port Moody was to be the terminus for the railroad and only changed after considerable debate in Parliament in Ottawa.

His was one of one hundred and twenty five signatures of the Petition for Incorporation. On April 6, 1886 a bill was passed in the Provincial Legislature creating the city of Vancouver. In my den hangs a copy of this petition - the original hangs in the foyer of Vancouver City Hall. I cherish this possession and important bit of history of our Province.

Later in the summer of 1886 a fire broke out in the new city known as the "Great Fire". It completely destroyed the young city including Herbert's home and possessions. It nearly claimed his life because he had collapsed in his attempt to escape the fire and was dragged to safety by a couple of strangers. However he did receive some burns to his face.

For a short time after the fire he served as a police constable and later as a councillor. Vancouver was his adopted city where he died many years later. He never did get back to his native Dorset.

Sophia Morehouse Fowler was born and raised in Upham, New Brunswick and moved with her parents, James Fowler and Agnes Humble. Many of the Fowler clan had settled in New Brunswick. They were originally from England and had emigrated to the New York area where they lived until 1776. They were there during the War of Independence which they vehemently opposed as they were devout United Empire Loyalists. Conditions became intolerable for those who opposed the war and when the Declaration of Independence was signed creating, what became the United States of America, the Fowlers left en masse for Canada - settling in New Brunswick.

The plight of the Loyalists is documented in a book entitled "The Loyalists of New Brunswick" written by Esther Wright.

Sophia and Herbert Ballson were married in 1895 and lived at what is now the Kingsway area. They had three children - the youngest being my mother, Celena, who was born in 1902.

Not too much is known about the first couple of years of Celena's life except that her mother died when she was four years old. Her brother, George, continued to live with his father but she and her older sister went to live with her grandmother in South Vancouver. In spite of the tragedy, my Mother describes her years there as happy times until her grandmother, whom she loved, died in 1911. At that time she and her sister moved back to live with their brother and father. Once again this small family was united as one. However this was to be shortlived because in 1913 her father died suddenly of a massive heart attack.

So as a result of this series of tragedies, my mother, at the age of eleven, became an orphan.

I often talked at length with her about this phase of her life which certainly was a sad episode. However she never did say too much about the sadness nor the sorrow but preferred to talk about the happy days with her grandmother and especially of the last year when she was again united with her family. I think these times had an important bearing on her philosophy of life in the future. At times when all was not going as well as it could, or when sad events happened, she would never look upon the dark side of issues but would always see something to smile about. This certainly applied as well to her opinions of people - never being critical and finding fault but always seeing and mentioning the good in them. It was a wonderful philosophy and the world would certainly be a happier place today if everyone were like her.

What was going to happen now? Her family was gone. Fortunately her father had appointed an executor who became a very trusted guardian for his children. His name was Mr. Fowler (no relation to the Fowler family described above). Also fortunately for the small family was that their father had invested well in property in the Vancouver area and was comfortably well off. So it was possible to send the children to a boarding school.

My Mother and her older sister were enrolled in All Hallows private school in Yale, B.C. The Anglican church had purchased the home and property of a Mr. Andrew Onderdonk who was in charge of construction of the C.P. railway as it pushed westward. The church had started an Anglican girls school on this site. After two years at this school my Mother went to live with an aunt in Vancouver where she attended King Edward High and later the Provincial Normal School where the graduates became teachers.

So in 1920 Celena had her teacher's diploma and accepted her first school on a place that she had never heard of before, called Denman Island. It is there that she met my father. After a year on the Island she taught at Westbank and Vernon in the interior of the province and in 1923 married Dad and settled on Denman.

I now propose to tell you about the Piercy family and my father. Irvine Piercy was born in Comox and grew up on

Denman Island. He was the youngest son of Thomas Piercy and Jane Speedy.

The first of the Piercy clan emigrated to Canada in 1837. They came from Northumberland in Northern England near the border of Scotland. Some of my Scottish friends tell me that there is a rumor that the Piercys were kicked out of Scotland because of stealing sheep. I have great difficulty accepting that anything of that nature would have been done in our family.

Quite a number of people were leaving Britain around this time because of the Corn Laws which were a number of measures and laws passed by parliament to regulate the supply of small grains (which the British called corn). These laws had been in effect since the 15th century and were supported by the powerful landlords in parliament. Basically these laws were to artificially elevate the price of corn so that they could collect more rent from the tenant farmers. But the high prices placed a very heavy burden on the poorer people of Britain. There was great pressure by the citizens to abolish these laws and because of poor harvests coupled with the potato famine in Ireland, these repressive laws were repealed in 1846.

Thomas Piercy and his wife, Mary and their five chidren were among a group that set sail from the Port of Berwick on May 28, 1837. They arrived in St. John, New Brunswick on July 12. He received a land grant of 100 acres in a place called Harvey in York County, N.B. just south of Fredricton. His oldest son, Matthew, my great grandfather, and his bride, Agnes accompanied him on the voyage. Other members of the Piercy clan were to follow in ensuing years. Thomas and Mary are both buried in the cemetery in Harvey.

Son, Matthew, and Agnes stayed in Harvey where they established a home and a farm and later a store and prospered very well. They became very active in community affairs and their church and they also found time to raise 12 children.

But he, like another grandfather of mine on my Mother's side of the family, had the urge for travel. After becoming well established and after 37 years in New Brunswick, he decided to move to British Columbia. Five of his daughters did not leave as four of them were married at the time. So with his wife, Agnes, five sons and two daughters they travelled by train to San Francisco and by sailing ship up the coast to Victoria. They then took a smaller ship up the east coast of Vancouver Island to the Comox Valley arriving in 1874. They preempted a large parcel of land just north of Courtenay where they again established a new farm. Vanier High School and the Community Pool-arena is located on part of this farm.

They became very active in community life and, of course, their church life. When they arrived here in 1874 there was no Presbyterian church so attended the Anglican church for a short time. One Sunday morning the minister asked the congregation to remain after the service as they had some business to deal with. Whereupon Grandpa Matt got up and stated that he had never done business before on a Sunday and was not prepared to start now. He led his family and friends out the door, gave part of his farm as a site for a new church and in 1876 a new church was opened. The church stands at the top of Mission Hill just north of Courtenay and is the site of a cairn constructed in 1974 to commemorate the arrival of the Piercy family in the Comox Valley one hundred years earlier.

Their family, like Matthew and Agnes, became quite

prolific and certainly did their part in populating this sparsely inhabited and isolated part of North America. Descendents of Matthew and Agnes meet here every five years for a family reunion and it is not unusual to have five or six hundred of the family together. The descendents of the five daughters in New Brunswick hold a similar gathering, usually two years after the Western clan meets. I had the opportunity to attend their last meeting in Harvey and seeing some of my Eastern relatives.

In the Piercy Family Tree book, which is constantly being updated, it is noted that as of 1997 there were 2098 descendents of Matthew and Agnes. I once heard a relative state that probably after the first two or three generations had passed away, the reunions would cease to exist because of lack of interest. Most of them in those generations have passed away and are no longer with us. Happily this is not happening because our clan reunions are increasing in size. I think it would be sad if we stopped meeting to remember our heritage as we do. People the world over, who are constantly searching for their roots, would love to be in our position.

Matthew's oldest son, Thomas - my grandfather who came west with him - was married at the time and had four children. He had married Jane Speedy in New Brunswick. She was from a large family that had emigrated from Britain. To me she became "Granny" Piercy and more later about her.

Thomas and Jane decided to settle on Denman Island. There the family acquired several hundred acres on the shore on the west side of the island looking across Baynes Sound at the Beaufort mountain range on Vancouver Island - a magnificent view. One of the reasons for establishing a farm at this location was the proximity to Union Bay - a deep, sea port on Vancouver Island just four miles from his farm and an ideal market for his farm produce.

Union Bay was a port where the ships on the west coast came for coal which was mined just a few miles away at the Dunsmuir mines at Cumberland. This remained a very busy coaling station until the 1940's and 1950's when ships began converting to oil as their fuel.

Thomas and Jane's property became a prosperous farm. In addition to a dairy herd and mixed farming they had planted an orchard with 1000 apple trees and other fruit trees. This wonderful orchard was planned to provide his retirement income - hoping to get one box of apples per tree.

This became known to all the relatives and islanders as the "Ranch". Here they raised their eleven children of which their youngest son was my father, Irvine. In the years to come he became the owner of this magnificent, picturesque "Ranch". And this is where I spent the early part of my life.

What an ideal place for a young boy to live. I have such wonderful memories of those young years and realize how fortunate I was.

As I write this I think of my children and their children and I realize that my great grandchildren are now the eighth generation of Canadians to live in this great country. It is my sincere hope that they realize this and share in a proud heritage that goes back over the years and realize the hardships endured by those ancestors and the effort they made to make a future for us in their adopted land.

MATTHEW PIERCY

CREST

HERBERT GEORGE BALLSON

SOPHIA FOWLER

THOMAS PIERCY

JANE SPEEDY

Chapter II

The Journey Begins

Travelling to and from Denman Island in the 1920's was not an easy matter. There was no such thing as a regular ferry service as it exists today. Using a rowboat to get to Vancouver Island was a common practice. Twice each week, the C.P.R. steamer visited the Island. Denman was on what was known as the triangle run which began in Vancouver with stops at Denman, Union Bay, Comox and Powell River on the mainland prior to returning to Vancouver. These fairly large ships were the life blood of coastal communities - delivering mail, food and supplies and leaving with farm produce destined for the city. They also carried passengers as they had quite a number of berths for overnight travel. A number of the C.P.R. fleet was used for this service and one such ship was the Princess Mary. The superstructure of this ship is in its final resting-place at the end of the Johnson Street Bridge in Victoria and became a well known restaurant.

Getting to a hospital from the Island was never too easy nor reliable unless planned and for this reason my mother traveled on the Princess Mary to Vancouver where she was to wait until her first child was born. After a few days, the waiting was over and on May 30, 1924 at 6 am a memorable event occurred and Irvine and Celena became the proud parents of their first infant son whom they later christened George Irvine. So in true Piercy custom they too had helped to populate the Comox Valley.

I was to have been born in St. Paul's Hospital but because of a staph infection in the nursery, the maternity floor was closed. I, therefore was born in a small private hospital on Thurlow St. in the west end of Vancouver.

Mothers did not walk back to their beds from the case room following a delivery in those days as they sometimes do at present. It was necessary and standard procedure to spend at least 10 days in bed without getting up. Medical history has shown that this practice, which was to continue for a number of years, was not in the best interest of the mother's health. Many mothers, because of this inactivity developed phlebitis - an inflamation in the veins of the legs and in those days it was referred to as "milk leg". Today early mobility has almost eliminated this serious problem.

In the following week my father came on the steamer to Vancouver where he inspected me, gave his stamp of approval amd decided to keep me for better or for worse. So at the age of 12 days, they let me loose on the world and I became a young passenger on the Princess Mary and saw Denman for the first time.

On arrival back on the island, we moved into the old Ranch House built in 1877 and owned by my grandmother. My father was in the process of building a new modern home on the same property that we moved into in the fall of 1924. Granny moved with us and for the first time the old ranch house was vacant. She became an important member of our family, living with us for the next 14 years until her death in 1938. She played an important role in my early life.

She was the only one of my grandparents that I ever knew and I often wondered just who the others were and wished that I could have known them. I had been christened George Irvine after my grandfather on my mother's side of the family and, of course, my father. In my early years Granny had shortened my name to Sonny and I was called that for a number of years in spite of my disapproval. However this did not diminish my close relationship with her. I adored her.

In the ensuing years our family began to increase. Two years after I arrived, my sister, Zeta, was born followed by my brother, John and later a second brother, Wes, thus completing our family. We all were very fortunate in that it was such a very loving, happy family and it was a busy household. Granny, being the matriarch of the family, was constantly visited by her children and grandchildren so we were certainly aware of our relatives at an early age.

My recollection of my early life on the ranch is quite clear. The place was always a hive of activity. My father was a successful farmer and was a busy man especially in the fall when the orchard was producing and he was marketing his fruit. We always had what was referred to as the "hired man" who lived in the old house and helped with the never ending chores on the farm. And, of course, there were always visitors to see Granny. In spite of all this activity my father always had time for his young family. He just lived for his family. Quite often he would take one of us on day trips when he was on farm business. At home, he was always showing us something different and explaining to us his involvement with his cattle, horses and the farm. He taught us how to fish and later, when we were older, how to hunt and use a gun. In the case of the latter, he was an excellent marksman and teacher of gun safety. I have mentioned about the large orchard on the farm. At the age of thirteen his father purchased a twelve gauge shotgun for him and gave him the task of keeping the orchard free of the black marauders that, over the years, caused thousands of dollars in damage to his fruit harvest. He became an expert at shooting crows and I'm sure that their population in this area would be tenfold had it not been for the gift to him as a boy.

This orchard, planted by my grandfather, was probably the largest on the coast with 1000 trees. It was in full production when I was growing up on the ranch and it is unfortunate that my grandfather did not live to see it at this stage. At a very young age we learned how to climb a ladder and take part in the harvesting of the fruit. I should mention that these crops played a significant role in the supplying of funds for the educational costs that were needed in my schooling.

We had acres of land and fields that became our playground and as we grew up, the adjoining foreshore and beach was where we explored, and in the summer, learned to swim. The fields, nearly always, had several deer grazing and pheasants crowing. In the forest, at the rear of our property, there was an abundance of grouse and in the ponds there were wild ducks. Eagles nested in high trees. Learning about all this wildlife and their ways was most interesting and educational.

Life on the Island was very, very different from life in an urban centre. Firstly, we did not have electricity and this did not change until the 1950's when the Premier, W.A.C. Bennett, decided to electrify the rural areas of B.C. We did acquire a Delco electric plant for the farm that produced our own supply of lighting. However, it was not powerful enough to operate appliances. Our toast was made in a rack that could be placed on top of the kitchen wood stove over the open fire. Depending on the type of wood we were using and the heat of the fire was what determined how much toast was burned to a black charred object each morning. My mother baked a lot of bread. Our radio was operated by two car sized batteries and the reception was never very clear.

Denman had a private phone system that served quite a number of residents for many years. Each phone had a battery for power and each subscriber had a different number of rings and the length of each ring varied. If anyone wished to call our home, they would turn the crank and give four long rings. My uncle Jim's number was four long rings and one short ring and so on. If my memory serves me correctly, the store was two short rings followed by a long ring. Conversations were not guaranteed to be confidential as anyone could lift their receiver and hear the latest gossip. One lady made a practice of doing just that. Everyone knew who it was because of a nervous cough that she had. Almost every day it was necessary for one caller or another to say "Mrs. Parnell, hang up the phone". This served the community very well. I was always amazed how well it worked because quite a number of glass insulators on the phone poles were missing. This, of course, was attributed to the accuracy and skill of some of the Denman boys with their slingshots. Of course I did not cause any of this damage because I was never that good a shot.

In the case of an emergency, one would ring one long continuous ring and everyone would answer. This emergency number was also used for a very different purpose in later years when the Island obtained a ferry service. It was used to inform the citizens if the Provincial Police car had driven off the ferry. It was a warning to those who had not licensed their vehicle to stay off the road!

We had one store on the Island, a general store that sold nearly everything that one needed. It even had an order office for clothing and shoes. What was not ordered from the Eaton's catalogue could be ordered from the store. It also housed the post office and it became the meeting place for citizens, especially at mail sorting time. A great many of the world's problems were solved around that old stove in the middle of the store. The building still stands in "downtown" Denman and has changed very little in appearance since it was built.

Church life was of great importance to my family. There were two churches on the Island, the United Church and the Anglican Church. My mother was an Anglican and my father, a Presbyterian. The Anglican Church did not meet every Sunday as did the United Church and it was felt that one should receive some Christian teaching every Sunday, so we became members of the United Church. So at an early age I was enrolled in Sunday School and later in Bible School. My mother, occasionally, would attend both churches on the same Sunday. The importance of developing a sound Christian philosophy was constantly stressed and I feel it has had an influence on my life both in medical practice and later in political life.

There was always a fairly active social life on the Island. We had a large community hall where most of this occurred. They had whist and bridge evenings, potluck suppers, dances, amateur concerts, public meetings, etc. In winter, the main part of the hall was used for badminton and basketball competition. Another spot for socializing was the Denman wharf on "boat days", which occurred twice each week. People would meet there to receive and ship goods. As a child I had my first ice cream cone there because the purser on the ship would permit us to come aboard for a few minutes to make our purchase. On an Island that had no refrigeration an ice cream cone was a treat that any child would always remember.

Times were prosperous in the late twenties. The Island had a large Sandstone quarry that shipped stone by barge for construction purposes. The old Vancouver Post Office was one of many buildings constructed with stone from this Denman site. This operation was eventually closed as it was learned that after a few years of weathering, the stone began to show streaking and discolouration.

Logging was an important industry. Several companies were involved with this, especially the Henry Bay Logging Co. that built a railroad that ran from Henry Bay on the northwest side down through most of the northern section of the Island. One of my earliest memories was when my father took me for my first train ride on this old steam engine to the end of the line where he wanted to show me what logging was all about.

They logged most of the northern and central portion of Denman. This area has, in my lifetime, regrown into a new healthy forest and today is being reharvested - to the revulsion of a lot of the present group of Islanders and I know that it will again grow a new forest. I trust that this present attitude will change and that tree growth will again be treated as a crop.

In my view, a young, vibrant forest has a far greater benefit for our environment than an old bunch of rotting and diseased trees. However, there is little point in me wasting my time trying to convert these fanatical environmentalists who continue to be so vocal about falling a tree.

The fishing industry was very viable at this time with a large cannery at the south end of the Island at Deep Bay. Fish were plentiful. Each year, usually after the haying season was over, my father would take a day off and go fishing to get our winter supply of fish. He would ask my mother how many bottles did she plan to preserve. There was never a question of getting fish but was a matter of how many were needed. Using an old rowboat and a hand line provided an interesting afternoon. How different fishing is today.

In the early days of logging on the Island they certainly didn't understand the importance of protecting fish habitat and caused problems that thankfully could not occur today.

Denman had two lakes on the Island - Chickadee Lake and a chain of lakes called Graham Lakes. These were ideal places for swimming as well as places where we could go trout fishing - wonderful, beautiful spots.

In my conversations with my Dad in his older years he informed me that when he was a boy he remembers that Chickadee Lake was where coho salmon came each year to spawn. That does not occur today in spite of efforts to make it a salmon rearing lake again. The reason for this sad state of affairs is, of course, the logging that occurred on the Island where stream beds were altered and blocked with debris. Thankfully the rules have changed and any effort that causes degradation of streams and rivers is a serious offence today.

As I have written above, I have no problem with logging and future harvesting of our forests but we must continue to enforce the rules for such activity.

The Island was primarily, however, an agricultural community with many small farms - many too small to be viable in modern times. Farming continued to have this important role in the economy until the second World War when many of the farm boys left to join the military forces and did not return to the land and today few of those established farms are still in existence. One exception is the old Piercy homestead where, in combination with another farm, it is operated today by my young brother, Wes, who, for the last 50 years, has been actively farming on this site. He is the third generation of the family to do so.

Other aspects of life on the Island were changing as well. In the early 1930's ferry service was started running from the Denman wharf to Buckley Bay. At first it would take three cars at a time. But this was a very important step. Electricity arrived on the Island in the 1950's and a modern phone system, a short time later. All of these changes - although not too significant by themselves - have changed forever the lifestyle and character of this rural area where I was raised.

I failed to mention that we had a two-roomed elementary school on the Island. My mother had taught there in 1921. During her life she was to continually stress the importance of education to her children and then her grandchildren. It was obvious to me that my wonderful carefree, playful and exciting preschool years were coming to an end. It was time, according to mother, to get started on the formal educational ladder. Her continuous urging and support would continue for the next twenty years.

Our new home- 1924

Baby George

Granny Piercy and "Sonny"

View from The Ranch

Grandpa Tom's retirement planning

CHAPTER III

Off to School

I started school in 1930. Up until that time there had been two teachers for the school. One room for grades 1-4; the other for grades 5-8. My mother had taught the primary grades when she was there in 1921. But in 1930 there was only one teacher - whether this was an early warning of the depression that followed in the next few years or some other reason, I did not know nor did I really care. All I knew was that I was given a desk for the year in a class of forty-nine. Yes, and I repeat, a class of forty-nine-in one room. Nine of that group were in grade one. The year of 1924 obviously had been a very productive year on Denman and could, I suppose, be compared to the baby boomer years following the second world war. The other seven grades had fewer in number and by the time it came to the last grade, there were few students because in those days it was about time to join the labour forces as most did.

Our teacher was a very formidable appearing soul who could, and certainly would, maintain strict order. One feature about her was her hair. It was dark and obviously very long because she could braid it and in some way wrap it around on the top of her head to form a flat surface, which to my small eyes seemed to be about a foot in diameter. I was always wondering just how she could do this without placing a flat weight on it for compression. I don't recall learning too much in the first few weeks as I spent most of my time studying this hairdo and looking out the window watching blue jays sitting in trees waiting for the school lunch hour when they received a pretty good meal of crusts and uneaten sandwiches.

I have often reflected on this year and wondered how a teacher could cope with lessons for eight different grades in a room with forty-nine students. I compare it with the class sizes of today, yet we managed to plod along throughout the year and I was amazed at how much we did learn. This, however was the last year of this circus and when I returned for the next grade we had miraculously found a second teacher.

The ranch was three miles from school. Some of the children had even a further distance to walk. School buses did not exist but I certainly don't think the exercise hurt us too much. Occasionally, on stormy days, my father would drive us-picking up kids along the way until the car was full. The roads were not paved and gravel roads were certainly not "shoe friendly". I can recall each year when we got a new pair of boots, we had to have hobnails pounded into the soles to protect the leather. These metal inserts prolonged the life of the shoe but did nothing to make the classroom, with its wooden floors, any quieter.

As I advanced year by year to another grade, I found school life more enjoyable. Looking back over those years I can recall many incidents that stand vividly in my memory and I'd like to relate some of those to you.

Our school had a furnace system in the basement but for some reason it was never used during my years there. Instead they had a large wood-burning heater in the centre of each room. The school board, each year, would give a contract to one of the senior boys to take on the job of getting to school earlier each day for the purpose of lighting the fire. The pay was two dollars a month and I happened to get this lucrative contract in my last year. These stoves served two purposes-one was naturally to heat the room and this was certainly true for those who sat in desks located near the centre of the room. Another purpose was to heat our milk or cocoa at lunch hour. A large pot of water sat on the stove and at recess we would deposit our bottles of drink in the water, to be warmed by noon. Quite often someone would forget to remove the cork from their bottle or to unscrew the lid on their jar. We would all, of course, be made aware of this because there would occur a horrendous explosion-sometimes of glass, but of milk or soup or cocoa that would even hit the ceiling. This was certainly welcome at noon. I am told that my mother, while teaching there, started this practice as she felt the children should have a warm drink with their lunch, and a warm drink was extremely beneficial and very much appreciated by those whose desks were in the periphery of the room away from the warmth of the stove.

Behind our school property was a fairly dense forest of fir trees and over the years the students had managed to build a log cabin from small trees in the area. This had a small oil barrel in it that served as a stove. At recess we could go out to the cabin and start a fire that would be quite warm by noon hour. Each of us had a pointed stick that we could use as a spit to hold our sandwich while we toasted it. Only the senior boys in the school could use it and it was a very chauvinistic club-no girls were allowed. Obviously our hormones had not yet kicked in.

During lunch hour we would sometimes have what we called a paper chase. One group would have about a ten minute start striking off through the forest-dropping bits of paper-usually of newspaper used for our lunch wrapper. Later it was the task of the other group to find them. Very occasionally the group got carried away and misjudged the time to return to be at school when the bell rang. This led to quite a number of detentions after school hours.

We did not have a gym nor any organized school activities programs. All activity was left to and controlled by the ingenious leaders in the senior classes. Certain activities had been passed down from years before and all seemed to have a specific time of the year or season in which they occurred. One such game, which I'm sure every kid who ever went to Denman School remembers very vividly, and probably thanks their maker that they survived their participation, was called "Duck on the rock". How it got its name or when it started is unknown to me but it was certainly continued as a tradition. In the centre of our school yard there was an elevated dome shaped granite rock about four feet across and almost a foot in elevation. Obviously they did not have bulldozers in those days or I'm sure this landmark would have not existed. The only equipment necessary to participate in this activity was a rock which could be up to four inches in diameter. Some were perfectly round like a cannonball and were prized possessions. One person was designated to place his rock on the larger rock and it was known as the duck. The owner was known as the keeper. All others stood behind a line about fifteen feet away. The object of the game was to have those standing behind the line to throw their rocks and try to dislodge the duck from the big rock. The next thing to do was to try and recover one's rock and get back behind the line in order to have another shot at the duck. However as long as the duck was in position, the keeper could tag anyone picking up their rock. If he were successful in tagging anyone, that person would then become the keeper. It was certainly in one's interest to get rid of the keeper's job and for health's sake get out of the firing line. But the exciting part was yet to come. If someone's missile hit the duck and knocked it off the big rock, everyone could scramble to pick up their rock without fear of being tagged until the keeper could replace the duck. This is when all hell would break loose because as soon as it was repositioned, those who had made it back to the starting line would begin firing again. This was like a war zone with four inch granite missiles and pieces of rock going in all directions.

It was always amazing to me that no one was killed or lost an eye. My mother, I guess was quite aware of Duck on the Rock because she often warned us not to play that game. It also surprises me that while I was there, it was never stopped by a teacher. I guess they rationalized that it was a good way of getting us to expend some of our energy.

Another popular game was called Nobbies. Two three inch lengths of rubber tubing-usually cut from a section of old radiator hose were tied together by a cord holding the pieces of tubing about six inches apart. A stick resembling a hockey stick was made from a branch of a tree. The blade was shaped at the end in a very sharp point and this was done so the nobby could be scooped from the ground and carried on the end of the stick. We became quite expert at doing this and passing the nobby to a teammate at quite some distance away as we moved down the field to try and score on the goalie. It was a poor man's substitute for lacrosse.

Not all of our games were particularly participant friendly. In the school basement was a large 45 gallon wooden barrel that was used during the week as a garbage receptacle and on each Friday this was rolled out into the schoolyard, dumped and the contents burned and the empty container was returned to the basement. We could take turns climbing into the barrel that would be placed on its side and spun around on the cement floor. I can recall when one poor unsuspecting soul was placed in this gyroscope and spun faster and faster only to be saved by the bell ending our recess. As he got out of the barrel his equilibrium was so out of synch that when he attempted to run for the door, he bounced off a wall that was 90 degrees off his intended course.

These were some of the activities and games that were probably unique to a very rural school setting. Activities after school hours were always interesting and could only happen in a rural area. I could write pages and pages about some of these happenings and would like to mention just a couple.

My sister, Zeta, was in the second grade behind me in school and we were the closest of friends and always together. We travelled to school together and walked home together. On one occasion on our way home, we decided to take a short cut through my uncle's farm which happened to border on the property where our community hall was located. To our amazement we came upon a cache-a case of beer hidden behind a partially hollowed out stump. There had obviously been a dance at the hall and drinking inside was just something unheard of at that time. However a little bit of drinking occurred on the Island although the ladies of the community would never acknowledge that their men did such a thing. Anyway, any liquor brought to the dance was stashed outside and was sampled when the men went out for a bit of fresh air. And so for some reason or another-either because of memory loss or from too much of the evil drink-he was unable to find his hiding spot. In any case, Zeta and I now had this find in our possession and decided to report this discovery to our father. So off we went on our merry way with our find. It just happened that we were met enroute by my uncle's eldest son, Tom, who was now a grown man. In a very serious discussion, he asked us what we were doing and persuaded us, of all things, that we should return this to its hiding place as he was sure the owner would be looking for it. So my sister, who was eight and I being ten, did the proper thing and obeyed his good advice.

However it seemed to us a bit strange that our cousin could be seen taking a parallel course and always keeping an eye on us. After depositing our booty in its original place, we reversed our course and went home.

To this day I am sure that my cousin enjoyed this beer.

Some years later I reminded him of this day and related my suspicions. He smiled and informed me that he would never have done such a terrible thing. Oh yeah!

Another incident that got the boys of my vintage in a bit of trouble was when we decided that we would create a small logging camp and pretend we were loggers. My good friend, Ray, was obviously the boss and decided that the site of this operation would be on the upper end of his father's property. This property extended from the flat land on the west side of Denman and extended to the top of a ridge of land that runs down the centre of the island. This was an ideal location as we could fall the trees and they would slide down the slope to the bottom of the hill where we would set up camp. The trees on this slope were second growth and were six inches in diameter.

All was going well, but only for a short time. Few people may not realize what a group of half a dozen 13 and 14 year olds can do in short order when they have axes and saws at their disposal. After our third weekend at this operation, this bare spot on the hillside was becoming noticeable from as far away as Vancouver Island. I think we were the origin of the phrase "clear cut logging". Sure enough, it was spotted and I won't mention some of the penalties that were to follow if we didn't cease and desist immediately.

By now it was about time to leave the Denman Island school and my sister would soon follow me. I now had two younger brothers in the same school - Jack and Wes - and I knew they would continue with the fun of traditional games and activities that we older ones enjoyed.

The eight years there had been fun filled, carefree days. At the time of leaving, little thought was really given of my friends that I had met and of our teachers who sincerely tried to teach us. It is only years later that it all comes back and makes us realize what we had and what a unique experience it was.

Much lay ahead that was unknown to us as we left. We were all to go in different directions. When we get together, we do not talk too much about those directions but about those fond memories, and that's the way it should be.

GEORGE WITH ZETA, JACK AND WES

DENMAN SCHOOL

CHAPTER IV

Leaving Home

There was no high school on Denman which meant that anyone that wished to continue with schooling had to leave home. Commuting to Courtenay or Comox or Cumberland was out of the question. Finding a place to board was not that easy and paying for that was out of the question for most. For that reason, as was certainly the case up until now, not a very high percentage of those leaving the Island school continued with their education. Continuing was not a simple matter.

My mother placed a very high priority on getting a good education so leaving school was not an option for me and a way had to be found.

In many ways I was happy about this as I was beginning to

enjoy school life but saddened by the fact that I would no longer be able to live at home except on vacations and the occasional weekend. So in 1938 I moved to Comox, a small unincorporated area about 25 miles away. I had been fortunate in finding a place to live where I could do some work in order to pay for my board. It was on a farm owned by an elderly couple. I milked a couple of cows morning and night, fed the chickens and cows and did many different chores that arose from time to time.

Comox High was a relatively small school. In 1938, there were 4 high schools in the district-Comox, Courtenay, Cumberland and Tsolum. This situation continued for a number of years into the future until the school board, in their wisdom, decided to amalgamate these into a central school in Courtenay. I never considered that this business of uprooting kids from their own area and bussing them to a central location was a particularly great idea. Pride in one's area and school is an important feature that is lost. But I'm sure the school board had what they considered a good reason. In more recent years this policy was reversed and Comox again has its High School.

Life in school was great. I became active with the athletic teams-track, basketball and softball and really enjoyed that phase of activity. Competition amongst the four High Schools was very keen and some pretty good rivalries developed. Our principal was an excellent teacher and administrator and a very fine man who certainly understood the problems of those now living away from home. My sister came to Comox two years later and lived in his home for her entire time at High School. He was later chosen to be the principal at the new central school in Courtenay.

During my second year I moved and lived with an elderly lady and became the handyman around her home with chores that included helping her with her shopping and looking after her garden etc. Unfortunately, she was unable to have me there for another year as she was moving.

During the latter part of my second year in Comox, I became quite ill with a strep throat infection. The sore throat cleared quite rapidly but I developed a complication of the infection called Rheumatic Fever. It is characterized by a high fever, swollen painful joints and can affect other organs of the body and in particular the heart which happened in my case. The treatment of this condition was the unhappy part-I was confined to bed for 2 1/2 months extending through most of the summer. Gradually, the symptoms of fever and sore, swollen joints disappeared and I felt well again but on examination, the Doctor discovered that I had a heart murmur with some damage. This didn't really strike home to me as I was back to my normal activities. I didn't know at the time this murmur was going to have a profound effect on my future. What mattered was the fact that I was out of bed. To confine an active 16 year old to bed for a long time is a terrible sentence.

Later in my medical studies I was to learn much about the complications of strep throat infections. Rheumatic fever is one example where organs are affected and the other is nephritis-an inflamation of the kidney leading to kidney failure. These two conditions were not a rarity in those days. Fortunately, they are almost unheard of today, thanks to the discovery of penicillin and its use in treating strep throat.

We were having a problem trying to find a suitable place to board as I returned to school. Finally my father and I moved a log cabin from Denman Island and put it in a field in Comox on property owned by a relative. The logs were about 5 inches in diameter and the seams were well caulked. The cabin was 6 feet wide and 9 feet long and had a wood burning stove and was very cozy even in the wildest storms. I ate my supper at a relative's home but made my own breakfast and lunch. This was my home away from home for the next two years. The cabin was demolished in 1998 to make room for a patio home development on Balmoral Avenue next to d'Esterre Gardens Senior's homes. When I left high school at the end of my fourth year, I jokingly told friends that I hoped this could be preserved as it may become a National Heritage site should I ever become famous. In spite of my years as Mayor of Comox in years to come, no one seemed to make this preservation a high priority. It has gone in the path of the bulldozer.

I loved all the teaching and instruction at Comox High. My academic standards continued to improve. I became involved with the student's council and served as its president. I was awarded the Osler trophy given to one student for scholastic ability and citizenship and sportmanship in their final year. This prized trophy is still awarded each year to one student at Highland. It had originally been given in memory of Pip Osler who was an outstanding young man who was tragically killed in a motor car accident on the Dyke while in his final year at Comox High.

In my second year at Comox High, war was declared by our country against Nazi Germany. I still remember that day in early September. I was at home on the farm in a shed making apple boxes in preparation for the harvesting season when my mother came to the shed to give me the news. A great deal goes through one's mind when one hears news of that nature. I could not continue with the box making but just sat under an old maple tree by the shed as thoughts of previous wars went through my head. I'm sure my mother gave a lot of thought to this as well. She had three sons that possibly would be actively involved. And it all became close to home because friends and acquaintances soon were signing up for military duty and leaving the area. In the next few years news of those missing in action or those who had been killed appeared in the paper. It gave us a lot to think about.

On holidays and occasionally on weekends I would return to Denman and I cherished those visits. My brothers were no longer the little kids they had been. Life on the farm was still wonderful. Granny was gone, having passed away in 1938 at the age of 93 leaving a great void in our lives. Those that I had gone to school with over there had gone in various directions. Some were now in His Majesty's uniform. The Denman of my youth, as I knew it, was slowly changing.

My time at Comox was rapidly coming to an end which was sad for me because I really got to love the place and years later would return to work and live there. The war in Europe was not going well for the allies in 1942 and one major defeat after another made news in the paper and over the B.B.C. radio broadcasts from London. I was at the ripe old age of 18 and knew there would be changes in store for my life. I was beginning to think about doing the honorable and patriotic thing and getting involved in the war. Decisions were going to need to be made shortly.

In June of 1942 I graduated from Comox High with honors. It was sad to say goodbye to the friends I had made and to my principal, Ted Richardson, whom I considered a good friend and counselor.

That summer I decided to go to work and took a job at a large shingle mill across Bayne Sound from Denman at a place called Fanny Bay. I used a small boat of my father's to get to work. It had a small Easthope motor in it and there was no clutch that meant when the motor started, the boat took off. Getting the thing started was a different matter. This was accomplished by spinning the fly wheel of the engine which resulted, quite often, in losing some skin off my fingers and certainly learning how to curse. But this was my transportation to and from work for the summer.

This turned out to be the worst summer of my life. I had never minded working and working hard - I had experienced that on the farm. But the working conditions were indescribable. It was a hot summer and the mill was hot, dusty and dirty and screaming saws were all around. I understand why those mill workers later became deaf as no hearing protection was available. We worked five and a half days a week and the pay was 40 cents an hour. I stuck around till the end of the summer and vowed never again to work in such a place. More importantly, it was the greatest incentive to make one continue with their education.

VISITING MY HIGH SCHOOL HOME - 25 YEARS LATER

Chapter V

College days

In September I enrolled in Victoria College which is now the University of Victoria. At that time the college was located in the old Craigdarroch Castle, built by Robert Dunsmuir who was the coal baron who controlled the mines on Vancouver Island. I decided to do this because I was still not old enough to be in the services.

I chose mostly sciences in my course as well as English and German. The sciences included Biology, Chemistry, Physics and Mathematics. At this point in my life I was undecided as to what I wanted to do as a career. I tended toward becoming a teacher, probably of science, although no firm decision on this.

Military activity was all around and at the college they had what was called the College Officer Training Program. I enlisted in the Air Force division of this program. If I were going into the Military Service I would hope to get into the Air Force. We had certain classes set aside for this training. Firstly, we had to learn to march which I didn't particularly enjoy. In the classroom we had courses on basic navigation, map reading, plane recognition, etc - all quite basic. We were given uniforms and were to wear a white patch in the front fold of our caps. I didn't particularly care for the military authority and rules, but after a summer at the shingle mill I didn't complain.

Towards the end of that term I applied to enter the Air Force and reported to the old Bay Street armory where the medical exams were conducted. After the usual routine of weighing and measuring me, taking a history of my health, reading an eye chart, finding out if I could tell green from red and pissing in a bottle, I was led by an old Corporal who I'm sure had been in the Boer War, into a rather cold, unheated room in the armory and told to strip. Shortly a rather plump surly looking balding man with a Hitler style moustache appeared. He was obviously the Medical officer and he proceeded to examine me. He really didn't seem too enthralled with his work and said very little as he went through his exam except to comment on my web toes. He finally got around to checking my heart and lungs which I thought was a bit more important than noting my toes. As he was examining my heart the expression on his face changed as if he had discovered gold. He began questioning me at length about my past health and informed me that I had a pronounced mitral valve murmur. I really didn't know the difference between that and athlete's foot at that time. He informed me my classification would not permit me to enlist. There have been a few surprises and shocks in my life but this announcement really hit home.

How dare this pompous little man have the audacity to suggest that I was not fit. The year before I was very active in competitive sports and in the previous summer I had worked like a slave throwing big blocks of cedar around in that dusty old mill. It certainly gave me cause to do some serious thinking and it was obvious he was not going to change his mind. In fact a second physician from the next room was asked to give a second opinion. In spite of my obvious great disappointment, I was very glad the examination was over because I was getting damn cold sitting there in my birthday suit.

So the year ended and I returned home and started to look again for a job but not at Fanny Bay. There was plenty of work as so many of the men were no longer in the valley. I managed to get work in a logging camp on Hornby Island - an adjacent Island on the Gulf of Georgia just a mile from Denman across Lambert Channel.

Hornby was a beautiful Island in the summer. A couple of the finest sandy beaches in B.C. lie on its shores. On the south eastern end was a beautiful peninsula overlooking the ocean and the famous Tribune Bay. This area is now preserved and is known as Helliwell Park.

There were quite a few tourists on the Island even in those days and quite a number of families spent their vacations there staying at the several guest lodges that existed. Some of them even brought their daughters and in addition to the girls that worked in the lodges we certainly had other interests besides earning a living.

I usually managed to get home on the weekends. The owner of the logging camp was a man from Denman whose first name was Caesar and the two of us would row across Lambert Channel each Friday night and return to Hornby on Sunday night. There was usually quite a brisk breeze blowing to hamper us so Caesar came up with the great idea that we should rig up a sail and in due course this was done. Neither of us had any knowledge of sailing. This masterfully built sail was only used once. On our maiden voyage we managed to get about 100 yards off shore when the boat flipped on its side and Caesar and I looked like two drowned rats. Enough of sailing.

This was an extremely enjoyable place to spend the summer and I was fortunate to be able to return to the same camp in the following two years. Caesar and I continued to return home each weekend by rowboat.

I returned to Victoria College in the fall and continued to enroll in a fairly heavy science program. Because of my abrupt rejection of my airforce application, I felt it would be a complete waste of time to continue in the College Officer's Training Course so took my demit.

I managed to get a weekend job to help defray expenses. I drove a delivery truck for a lumber yard on Government Street. The amazing thing about this was that I managed to finish the year without having an accident. This was probably a very good thing because I didn't possess a driver's license.

I lived for part of the year with a family that had moved from Bamfield on the west coast of Vancouver Island. The father remained there at the wireless station. He had moved his family to Victoria following a shelling attack on the station by a Japanese submarine. This never recurred but was a reminder that the war was in full swing and quite close to home.

At the end of this year I received a brown envelope in the mail from the Ministry of Defense in Ottawa. It was a polite request to take the forms they sent and report to a physician for examination in preparation for induction into the Army. I had reached the age when I was required to do this. It became quite clear that one branch of the service had not been informed of the findings of my previous attempts to wear a uniform. From my brief, short time in the COTC, I had had a bit of marching to do and thoughts of long army marches did not particularly enthuse me. In fact I had really stopped thinking about doing the patriotic thing and serving my country.

So I proceeded to make arrangements for another examination. The findings of my previous two examiners were confirmed on this examination as well and I was given a rejection category. I was never to hear from Ottawa again until I started to pay Income Tax.

The rheumatic fever that had caused all this rejection never recurred as quite often happens and the valvular damage that caused the murmur gradually, over a prolonged time disappeared completely. I am very thankful for that.

What was I going to do for the rest of my life? It was time to get down to some serious planning. These decisions are not easily reached and may change a number of times before one settles into their lifetime vocation. I had once wanted to get into teaching and this was still a possibility but because of some courses I had taken - Biology and Zoology especially - I began to have thoughts about medicine.

Because of my biology and zoology courses I was hired by the Pacific Salmon Treaty Commission. This was a joint venture by Canada and the Americans that studied and regulated quotas for salmon catches on the Pacific coast. Their headquarters were located in New Westminster. My job was to spend part of the summer in the lab doing some research or so they called it. The rest of the summer was to be spent at Hell's Gate on the Fraser River counting and tagging sockeye salmon. In the lab I had the very scientific job of looking through a microscope all day counting the rings on salmon scales. These samples of salmon scales had been scraped from the bodies of the salmon in the previous year. Each year a salmon grows a new ring on their scales and by counting these rings one could determine the age of the fish as it returned to the river to spawn. Well, the maximum number of rings that I saw was four and doing this for 8 hours a day for 2 weeks was enough to send me around the bend. I never did get to Hell's Gate to collect scales for the scientist to count in the following year because after I received my cheque on pay day I quickly headed for the ferry on my way back to the Island and my old friend Caesar who was still logging on Hornby. This was the first and last time I held down a government job.

Victoria College offered only two years of instruction so to continue with my studies I enrolled at the University of B.C. in Point Gray. U.B.C. was quite different, mainly because of its size and lack of fellowship noted at Vic college. I again continued with a heavy curriculum of science courses. I seemed to spend most of the week in the laboratory. Bacteriology, Chemistry, Zoology, Physics were the main courses and by now I was really thinking seriously about medicine.

British Columbia did not have a medical school at that time

and as it turned out didn't have one for another 15 years. The nearest school was in Edmonton or Winnipeg. I was impressed by what I had learned about the older established schools. I chose to put an application into McGill University in Montreal and a friend of mine was doing the same thing. It may have been an exercise in futility as my year at UBC was only my third year and McGill usually only accepted graduates with four years of university. Anyway I sent in my application and continued with my courses.

One of the exciting experiences that I would have while going to UBC was my trip from Kerrisdale where I boarded with my uncle and his family, a distance of 10 or 15 miles. A chap from Courtenay was also attending UBC and he had a motorcycle. Rather than pay streetcar fare I chose to make this trip with Roger. He only knew one speed - full steam ahead. What a ride. We didn't even wear helmets in those days and how we survived that ride I do not know. I turned prematurely gray like my Mother and I'm sure this transportation system played a role.

The year at UBC passed uneventfully and was rapidly coming to an end. One afternoon I was sitting in the living room at my uncle's home, listening to a news flash announcing the sudden death of President Franklin Roosevelt. It was April 12, 1945. He ccrtainly was a victim of the war. The responsibility which he had borne over the duration of the war must have been almost unbearable. This great man was gone and his nation was in mourning. The war in Europe was winding down and a victory after 5 terrible years was in sight. How long the Pacific conflict with Japan would continue was uncertain.

While I was listening to the radio the mail man brought our mail and in it was a letter addressed to me from McGill University. I was almost sure I had been rejected but to my great delight I read that I was to report on September 5th of that year for registration in the first year Medical course. I just couldn't speak because of such a surprise. I had been doing very well scholastically and my high grades had obviously taken precedence over the requirement of a degree for admission. Rationing was still in full swing in Canada but my uncle gave me his liquor ration coupons for that month and with my friends we had a few drinks to mark the occasion.

What a memorable day and what an important letter. In a few weeks I would celebrate my 21st birthday. I had just been given a key to my career and I certainly felt privileged.

It was now a summer of waiting and thinking of becoming a real doctor. So I returned to Hornby Island for my last session of work there. My weekends at home took on a far greater significance because I knew that it probably would be several years before I could be with my family again. My sister had married and my two brothers were approaching adulthood and would reach that stage while I was away, and the ranch was still as beautiful as ever.

The thought of leaving all this and going to a strange part of the country was almost scary but any fears were allayed by my Mother's encouragement and her desire to see me complete my education. My Dad was a fairly quiet man and didn't show too much emotion but I could tell that he was very proud of that little kid that he had brought home from Vancouver on the Princess Mary when he was 12 days old.

VICTORIA COLLEGE

AT MY DESK - THINKING ABOUT STUDYING

THE RODDICK GATES
ENTRANCE TO MCGILL CAMPUS

CHAPTER VI

Montreal and McGill

It was Sept. 1, 1945. The long summer of waiting was over and it was time to move on. Earlier in the summer I had celebrated my 21st birthday and in May the armistice was signed ending the terrible conflict in Europe. That chapter in our lives was over and an elated public was slowly returning to normal.

After saying goodbye to my family and friends, my Mother and I travelled to Vancouver where she and my uncle George watched while I went through a gate onto the platform of the CPR railroad. As the train pulled out of the station I realized that a new life was beginning for me.

The trip to Montreal would take five days. The cars were all quite old and certainly were in need of upgrading. They were noisy and actually quite dirty because the windows were not air tight and a lot of soot would gather on the sill by the end of the day as the locomotives were fired by coal - not diesel oil like today. But all of that did not matter. I had never been further east than New Westminster so every new vista was interesting to me.

As we travelled up the Fraser Canyon into the interior of the Province the change of scenery was certainly a contrast as we left the lush, green coastal area and entered the arid areas of the interior. And then came the magnificent Rocky Mountains. As we progressed up each valley and rounded each turn the view of a different mountain appeared. I thought we had some pretty big hills on Vancouver Island and the coast but these magnificent, towering rocky peaks, some of which were covered with snow or glaciers, was awe inspiring.

As we continued into the foothills of the Rockies we entered the cattle ranching area of Alberta. Next came the vast flat lands of our prairies where one could look out over miles of waving, yellow wheat fields. As we passed through the many small villages, each had several grain elevators beside the tracks waiting for the harvest to arrive. It was harvesting time and the threshing crews were in full swing. My thoughts were on the years when many young men from all over Canada would head for the prairies to take part in this activity. Back home on the "ranch" our fields were always quite small. These were quite different, extending as far as the eye could see. It was a magnificent sight.

On the night we arrived at the head of the Great Lakes they were experiencing an electric storm. Having grown up where these storms are rare and one may just see one or two flashes of lightning, I was in for a spectacular night. As the train rolled on we could not hear the thunder but hour after hour the sky was bright with flashes.

Heading into Northern Ontario was so different. This was really a rocky, uninhabited land with thousands of lakes and swamps that abounded in wild life. It was here that I saw my first moose standing knee deep in a muskeg, eating and not paying much attention to the train as we passed along. This became a common sight.

Before long we were entering the flat land of Quebec. One feature that stood out was the width of the small farms. I learned later that originally these farms were much larger - usually a quarter of a section - but over the generations strips of land would be subdivided and given to one of the family. I actually saw some parcels of farm land no wider than 100 yards extending back about half a mile, each with a home at the front of the property. This manner of subdividing off a piece of property was strange to me and so different from what I had seen where the parcel subdivided could be any shape. It was obvious that they used the frontage of the property as a measure of the size. We passed through many small village, each with its church in the centre. The church spires could be seen for miles as we would approach each village. Then we crossed the bridge onto Montreal Island and were shortly in this great city of which I would learn a great deal about in the next four years.

This trip across Canada, with its very different regions, was an enjoyable experience and gave one a lot to think about. To me, it made me very proud of this vast land of ours and very happy to be a Canadian. With this great resource I knew that the future for us was unlimited.

During the trip I found that most of the meals in the dining car were quite expensive so I ate sparingly, waiting until I got to Montreal where I was sure they could beat the CPR rates. So as I left Windsor station onto the streets I spotted a restaurant called Mother Martin's. It was in a very old building as most were in this older section of downtown Montreal. I was carrying an old well worn suitcase with some of my worldly possessions - the rest were to arrive in an old trunk later. Carrying this old case and in need of a good shower after 5 days of travel across Canada, I'm quite sure I looked like an immigrant just off the boat from war torn Europe. I wandered into this old restaurant looking forward to a very filling meal. I was rather surprised that the tables were covered with white linen and the menu was given to me by a waiter in a tuxedo. I began to wonder about all this especially for the first time in my life the different choices in the menu had no prices beside them. Shortly a violin player appeared at my table and began to serenade me. I had never seen anything like this on Denman Island and very quickly picked up my old suit case and cleared out. I later learned, of course that this was one of Montreal's world famous restaurants. You live and learn and if I wanted to act uppity I could say that I had been to Mother Martin's.

During the summer new medical students from out of town were sent letters by the two medical fraternities at McGill inviting us to visit them when we arrived.Their reason for this letter was 2 fold. First they genuinely wanted to offer help in finding accommodation and introducing us to the University - the other, of course, was to size us up and see if they wanted to invite us to join their fraternity. Both were on University Street. So after my exodus from Mother Martin's I began the long hike up University Street where I was warmly welcomed and given advice on where to go for accommodation. They did find a room for me on the third floor in a long row of buildings on Rue Jeanne Manse. Each was touching each other and each had an exterior staircase to the various levels of the building. My first thought was if I ever were out for a night on the town and had too much of Molson's brew, I probably never could find my way home because they all looked the same.

I spent 2 weeks in this attic room and in the interval one of the fraternities known as Nu Sigma Nu had time to think about me and invited me to join them. I did this and it was learned that there was a vacancy in the fraternity house for one more live-in member. I certainly was pleased to accept this offer and happy to move before an ice storm hit because I'm sure I could never have descended that spiral staircase if it was slippery.

The fraternity house, known as the Nu Sig house, was able to accommodate 14 members plus a room in the basement for our caretakers, a couple who did our cooking and took care of the washing and cleaning. It was a large older home owned by the University and rented by us. It was ideally located for a home for medical students - across the street from the Royal Victoria Hospital where we would later receive a lot of our clinical training and a block away from the medical building on the McGill Campus. I think this was one of the most important moves I was ever to make and I lived in this house for my four years while in training.

As I stated, all of our members were medical students sharing our common problems and helping each other. We were from all parts of Canada and the United States. We had a couple from England and two or three from the Carribean.

Those members of the fraternity that lived in the Nu Sig house became a closely knit group. We got to know about each others past, about our likes and dislikes and about our habits. We shared each others notes, our text books and what we had learned that day. Our evening meal was usually an intellectual experience and all sorts of subjects were discussed and debated as the fourteen of us gathered in the dining hall.

On occasion we even shared each others clothes which brings to mind a very amusing event. On one occasion one of the fellows needed a tuxedo in order to attend his girlfriend's graduation ball. He was of a short, stocky build. His room mate, who was quite tall had a tux that fitted him quite well except the pants were too long - no problem. He took them down the street to a tailor to have them taken up about 6 inches. Whether it was due to a language difference or whether his instructions were not clear enough will never be known, but the tailor cut 6 inches off the bottom instead of just taking them up. This was not discovered until a later date when the owner of the tuxedo needed his suit. I can still hear the laughter when he came into the sitting room one night to show us the sad appearance of his pants.

We were a hard working group but usually on the weekend - unless there was an impending exam - we certainly relaxed. Saturday night was usually a house party and we all have fond memories of those affairs. However we were constantly aware that we were members of a class of 120 that the faculty had chosen from a list of hundreds and they expected each to be worthy of this selection. Any failure to meet their high academic standard usually brought swift and often final censure.

As one of the junior members of our fraternity I was put on a wagon patrol. Rationing of beer was still in effect even though the war had ended. In Montreal one had to buy groceries in order to get an allocation of beer as all beer was sold in grocery stores. Each week our house received quite a large grocery delivery in which we received a generous allocation. However it was never quite enough. So each Saturday two or three of us would make the rounds of the corner grocery stores in our area towing our wagon like little boys, hoping to return with a few groceries and more Molson's ale. There was also a sled in the basement that could be used in the winter but the rationing ended so I never got to experience that.

After finding a place in which to live I was given a brief tour of the campus by one of the fellows in the fraternity. This was to familiarize me with some of the locations where I would be studying and of which I would get to know very well. The first place I would see was the Medical Building located on the upper and highest part of the campus. This very large and impressive building did stand out because of its unique architecture and ivy covered walls. And as I walked down the pathways I was impressed to see so many of these grand old structures - some named after some benefactors of the University or some renowned person who was associated with McGill's evolution or its teaching. There was the MacDonald Engineering Building, the Redpath Library, Douglas Hall, Molson Stadium, etc. There was a building for nearly every faculty - Law, Arts, Architecture, Theology, and the list goes on.

The old Roddick Gates on Sherbrooke Street still stand at

the entrance to this campus. As one enters through these gates onto the tree lined paths that wind among those famous buildings, one is struck by the quietness and solitude, in spite of being surrounded by this large city. McGill's beauty comes from its location and its character. As one looks up this sloping campus the buildings seem to grow out of Mount Royal that rises from its upper boundary. It is truly a beautiful, exciting campus.

As I strolled along, my thoughts were on the thousands and thousands of students that had wandered through those doors over McGill's long history. I thought of the famous teachers and professors that had lectured there and of the research and discoveries that had originated in these halls. I also wondered about the many graduates who left here for places and careers all over the world.

But the one thing that went through my mind was the fact that I too was entering this procession of students and hopefully one day would graduate. It was a challenging thought.

What was the origin of this McGill? How and why did it become located on this particular place? For those answers we must get to know a little bit about the man whose dream finally was realized.

James McGill was born in 1744, the son of a blacksmith in Glasgow. The fact that he left Glasgow University shortly after entering at the age of 12 showed that hard times had fallen upon the family and his father could see no great future for him in Scotland. He was barely in his teens when he and his younger brother left home and emigrated to North Carolina to be with relatives.

Meanwhile the last of the colonial wars between Great Britain and France ended. Quebec fell to the armies of General Wolfe on the plains of Abraham in 1759 and in 1763 under the terms of the treaty, France ceded all of New France to the British and it became a British province.

McGill, at the age of 19, came to Montreal to look around and in the fur trade he saw a chance for himself. For a considerable time in his early life he became a voyageur - travelling by canoe up the rivers into the interior of the country even reaching the Mississippi River - all in search of furs and especially beaver pelts. It is stated that he learned the fur trade from the bottom of his canoe to the head offices in Montreal. He formed a partnership and formed the North West company, giving up his life on the river for an office in Montreal. They became involved in receiving furs from the voyageurs for shipment to England and receiving goods in return to keep the trade alive.

Meanwhile the American Revolution was underway and he, as a very prominent member of the merchants of Montreal, helped to form a militia to defend the city which they did successfully thus helping to keep Canada in the British camp. He later became a member of the Canadian Committee which petitioned the King for an independent constitution and responsible government in Canada.

He lived on the Burnside estate on the side of Mount Royal and sloping down toward the city of Montreal. This picturesque setting would later become the McGill campus. He had a keen interest in education. In his writing he describes how he did not know of a single school for teaching boys in the whole district and lamented the fact that only one man out of five could read or write.

Agitation for schools mounted and the Home Government in England in an attempt to appease the reformers, created the Royal Institution for the Advancement of Learning. This institution really only existed in name and little happened. In 1811 James McGill performed one of the most important acts of his lifetime. He wrote his will and deliberately framed that document so that it might be used by his executors as a goad to stir the community into action. To the Royal Institution he bequeathed in trust the sum of 10,000 pounds together with his Burnside estate of 46 acres for the sole purpose of creating a university on his property and it was to bear his name. He also stipulated that the University must be established within 10 years after his death. Failure to do this would cause the bequest to revert to his other heirs.

He died 2 years later in 1813 and was buried in the Protestant Cemetery where his tomb stone stood until 1875 when it was moved to the campus and placed near the steps of the arts building.

After some difficult years and including a law suit by one of his heirs, the Royal Institution received a charter for the University granted by King William IV in 1824. After the opening ceremonies in 1829 the Board of governors held a historic meeting with the Montreal Medical Institution which had been established in 1823. They taught medicine to a few students at the old General Hospital. The purpose of this meeting was to engraft this institution to the University as the Faculty of Medicine. This was the first faculty established at McGill giving it the honor of being the senior faculty. It was also the first medical faculty in Canada.

And all of this campus that I was seeing was in the heart of Montreal - probably one of the most interesting and exciting cities on the continent. Montreal was a bustling metropolis and Canada's largest city and was located on an island. It was the centre of trade and commerce for the country with its corporate offices that controlled most of the business. It was a deep sea port at the end of the Gulf of St. Lawrence and the point where later the seaway from the Great Lakes ended. Canada's major railways had headquarters here. It was a very cosmopolitan centre with so many cultures and nationalities and predominently French. Their roots were of historical significance and reflected in the many interesting things to see, especially their churches and shrines. It was a city that was alive both day and night.

One of the regrets I have after my four years there was that I did not become fluent in the French language. I was in an English speaking university as was also the case of the hospitals in which I trained and there was little opportunity in that setting to learn and speak the language.

NU SIG HOUSE - MY HOME FOR FOUR YEARS

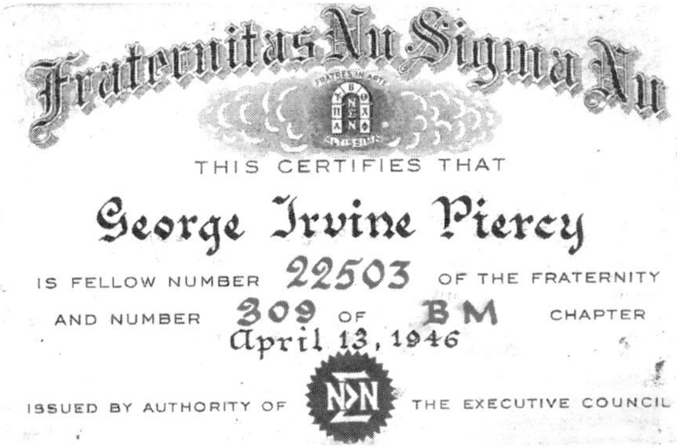

Fraternitas Nu Sigma Nu

THIS CERTIFIES THAT

George Irvine Piercy

IS FELLOW NUMBER 22503 OF THE FRATERNITY

AND NUMBER 309 OF BM CHAPTER

April 13, 1946

ISSUED BY AUTHORITY OF THE EXECUTIVE COUNCIL

WITH DORIS AT THE MEDICAL BALL 1947

CHAPTER VII

Medical School

In the early part of September I reported to the office of the Dean of Medicine where his secretary met and greeted me and saw that I was enrolled and given schedules of what I would be doing for the next few months. Included was a list of text books that I needed and the type of microscope I should purchase and she wished me well.

Her name was Miss Mudge. She was a great friend of all the medical students. There was little that happened in the Faculty that she was not aware of and she had a great deal of input into the department's affairs. I often wondered just how much she had to do with the selection process from the many applications for admission to medicine that they received each year.

Our class consisted of 120 students which was the usual size for McGill. We were joined as we started our second year by another 40 veterans who began their study in January and carried on through the summer vacation. They were, as a rule, older students that had returned from the war. Some had been about to start their medical course prior to the war and were now resuming their studies.

At the start of our third year 4 or 5 came to us from the University of Saskatchewan where they only offered 2 years of instruction. Students there had to complete the course at other facilities across the country. A few of our number did not pass their exams successfully and left us at various intervals but we ended up with about 155 in our graduating class which was the largest number in McGill's history. Of that number we had 6 female members - quite different from today.

After registration I proceeded to look around the corridors of this immense medical building. There were quite a number of fairly large class rooms, one very large room where individual desks were set up and where examinations were held, offices, laboratories, a medical library and on the third and top floor was the anatomy lab. Upon reading my schedule I learned that I was to meet here on the following day which I did and was put in a group of 6 students. Each group was assigned a cadaver that would keep the group's attention for 9 months.

The library in the medical building is known as the Osler Library - named after one of McGill's most famous medical graduates, Sir William Osler. During his lifetime he served as a professor in John Hopkins University and in London, England and he became, probably, the leading physician in the world. A record of his many medical writings and his discoveries and his teachings is housed in this library. Because of his great work, he was knighted during his term in England.

During the first year in medicine anatomy is the main course. On six mornings a week from 8:30 till noon our group would carefully and painstakingly dissect the body before us - learning the course of every nerve and blood vessel and tendon and the position of every square inch of the body in relation to every other structure around it. This dissection was done along with formal lectures on that part of the human frame on which we were working.

Our afternoons were spent on formal lectures and demonstrations on a number of subjects usually related to the normal functions of the body and the appearance of normal cells and bacteria found in the body - physiology, histology and bacteriology. Organic chemistry was the only course not taught in the medical building so we had to go elsewhere on campus to the chemistry building.

This was our daily routine for 5 1/2 days a week and at the end of the day it was an evening of studying. There was little time to think of anything except medicine.

During my first Xmas vacation I spent the holiday at the fraternity house as a trip back to B.C. was out of the question. I would like to relate a conversation I had with one of my classmates while we were there together. He had come to Canada from England just before the declaration of war and didn't get back. He began telling me how in 1938 he saw a demonstration of a machine that could receive pictures over the airways. The British had invented, in the mid thirties, what was later to be known as Television. I had never heard of this and listened in disbelief as he would repeat the story to me. At times I even wondered if he was having hallucinations. It was still another four years before I saw my first T.V.

At the end of my first year a classmate informed me that he was going to Jasper to work in the CNR hotel there. It turned out that his father was the architect that designed this famous lodge and that he was sure he could get me a job, which he did. The lodge, each summer, would hire students to work there during the busy tourist season. It always was an enjoyable time for students. I was there to be a caddy on the golf course but I soon learned that depending on tips was not a very certain way of earning money for the next year's books and supplies. I had been assigned by the caddy master to a young medical interne from the Mayo Clinic who was there with his wife on their honeymoon. More important to me, I soon learned that he was about as poor as I was because after one week of toting his heavy golf bag, he gave me 5 dollars.

So I switched jobs and began working in the store room filling orders for the various requisitions that came from the hotel kitchens and dining rooms. Our return fare on the CNR was only guaranteed if we stayed the summer. I still didn't get back across the Rockies but did have an enjoyable time at this beautiful lodge in the foothills of those mountains.

During that summer a fringe benefit was meeting Bing Crosby who was staying at the Lodge while they were producing the movie "Emperor Waltz", in which he played the leading role. In the evenings he occasionally would drop in at the staff dining and activity centre and sing a few songs for us. I also often watched him practicing his golf shots and can say that he was a pretty good golfer.

Before too long we were back for our second year and glad to see each other again. Classes started in earnest right away. The first half of the year consisted mostly of lectures relating to changes in the body that occurred following insults such as infections, tumors, conditions relating to the aging process and so on. We learned the effect these had on the appearance of the cells and organs of the body and the changes in the body chemistry. We had lectures on internal medicine learning the history of certain conditions and the symptoms they caused and the signs that we were to find on examination. It was becoming extremely interesting and fascinating and we began to realize that after so many years of prepartion we were beginning to really find out about medicine.

In February of our second year we reached an important milestone. We were about to begin our clinical training which meant entering the hospitals and getting to see what illness was all about. It meant examinations of patients and having an opportunity to relate to them. It also meant that we had matured enough to carry a stethoscope - which certainly built our ego and gave us a feeling of being very important.

We had a number of hospitals - all English speaking - at our disposal. Close to the medical building was the Royal Victoria Hospital and in the older section of the city was the Montreal General. The Children's Hospital was a short distance above the University. We also had access to the Protestant Mental Hospital in Verdun and Queen Mary's Military Hospital. Some of our lectures were held in Wilder Penfield's Neurological Institute or in the Allen Memorial Institute. We were to spend a great deal of time in our final years at these landmarks.

Another very important event happened in my second year

and had nothing to do with medicine. Early in the fall of 1946 I met a beautiful young coed who was attending McGill and training to be a physiotherapist. Her name was Doris Sturgess. Doris grew up in Montreal and knew the area very well . As the year wore on we were seeing each other with increased frequency and enjoying each others company very much. It was becoming obvious to me that I was falling in love with this lovely chick.

At the end of my second year I had an opportunity to return home to see my family. A classmate was going to pick up a new car in Detroit and deliver it to his father in Vancouver. I quickly accepted his offer for a ride. After taking possession of the car a fairly uneventful trip ensued except while driving through Wisconsin. We discovered that the gas tank had sprung a leak. So after a couple of days in Madison we were able to continue. This repair job used up most of our travelling money making it necessary to use the car as our motel room for the rest of the trip.

How happy I was to be back on the farm. Mother and Dad looked just the same. My sister was now a mother and I was an uncle. Jack was enrolled at UBC in agriculture and Wes was starting his career as a farmer.

It was a summer of seeing old friends and catching up on all of the events of the last two years. The farm, with its view of the ocean and of the mountains, was as beautiful as ever. As I sat behind my desk in Montreal I often thought of this very scene. The weather was wonderful that summer. I worked at a few jobs that vacation - including several weeks spent painting the Denman ferry. But it all came to an end too quickly. I was aware that I would not be home again until I had graduated which I must accept. So I was soon back on the train heading for McGill and Doris.

Our third and fourth years were extremely busy ones. The day would usually start quite early on the hospital wards where we would meet and listen to and examine patients. We would be in small groups of 5 or 6 accompanied by a physician acting as our tutor, or we might have a professor with us. We would be on a rotation basis, moving from one type of ward, eg, a surgical ward to a maternity ward on the following week. On the next week we might find ourselves in the Children's Hospital.

In this way we got to meet our professors and learn of their experience in treating a particular problem patient. Some were well known and renowned in their particular field such as the famous neurosurgeon, Wilder Penfield, the man responsible for building the Neurological Institute. Jonathon Meakins, our Dean, had written his book on Internal Medicine which was used by students all over North America. Others like Lyman Duff of pathology, Alton Goldbloom of Paediatrics, Griffiths in anaesthesia and Hans Selye who proved that stress caused pathological changes in the body were a few of the names that received recognition for their work throughout the world. It was such an honor to have met them and to have received part of our training under their guidance. Our afternoons were usually spent back in the lecture halls where so many different subjects were taught. We even had lectures on medical conditions that some of us possibly would never see such as in our course on tropical medicine.

We had lectures on therapeutics where we learned about the medications available for each condition and the dosage that would be prescribed. It was an exciting time in medicine as new drugs were discovered and prescribed. This was particularly true with the new antibiotics. I can recall when aureomycin, the forerunner of the Tetracyclines, was prescribed by our Professor in an experimental trial for the first time on a very ill young lady on our ward with pneumonia. She had not responded to penicillin therapy and was dying. The result was a dramatic and rapid recovery. It was quite an experience to see this drug used experimentally not knowing what the outcome would be.

After my third year I spent my first summer vacation in Montreal where I had a job working in the laboratory of the Montreal Neurological Institute. It was certainly not a very responsible job and I'm sure the place would not have folded if I didn't show up for work but I was always able to say that I had worked at this famous institution founded by Wilder Penfield, the world renowned neurosurgeon. During that summer I had time to visit some of the wards in the Royal Victoria Hospital which was an adjoining building so it was not a summer divorced from medicine.

Doris had graduated during that summer and was now working for an orthopaedic surgeon. We were still seeing each other frequently and in that fall we became engaged, and it was time to start thinking about our future together.

After the Xmas break we were nearing the end of our time at McGill. When we had started four years before, the end of our courses seemed eons away and I'm sure many of the class felt as I did that it would never end. As I reflected back on this chapter in my life I was amazed at just how quickly it really had passed.

The overall picture of medicine was now becoming clear to us. All of the subjects that we had been taught, all of the hours spent in labs, and all of the demonstrations that we had witnessed were like pieces of a giant jigsaw puzzle falling into place to form this total picture that made sense. Certainly we all realized that we had had a wonderful training in medicine and it was a recognized fact that McGill had one of the leading medical faculties in the world. If anyone in the class didn't learn a great deal, it was certainly not the fault of the professors and faculty members.

It was also patently clear that I was going to leave behind the many good friends I had made in Montreal. This was particularely true of the fellows I had met in my medical fraternity and especially those who lived in the Nu Sig House with me.

During those years my closest friend was a classmate and a member of the fraternity by the name of Elliott Young. He was a native of Montreal and lived with his widowed mother. Elliott had been in the RCMP but left after a couple of years to study forensic medicine which was becoming a very important work in the police arsenal in solving crime. It was his intention to return to the force to work in their laboratory for criminal investigation. We became very close friends - studying together, double dating together and even skipping a few boring classes together. He was the best man at our wedding and we named our only son George Elliott. While doing post graduate work in pathology in Boston he was taken into the U.S. army and sent to Korea where he spent 2 years in a mobile army service hospital (M.A.S.H.) After his discharge he became a pathologist and remained in New Hampshire. We visited each other on quite a number of occasions and sadly he died shortly after his 50th birthday. I miss him a great deal.

Our final exams - oral and written - began in May and continued daily for two weeks. The moment of truth was here! Usually one realizes just how well one has done when the exams are over and I felt quite confident that I had passed all of them. However I did not expect the good news that I received when I went to the Dean's office to get my results. To my surprise I had ranked sixth in our class of 155 and that I had led the class in surgery - winning the Robert Forsythe Prize in that subject.

Graduation date was set for the following week and on May 30th 1949, my birthday, I became George Piercy M.D.

My mother, fortunately, was able to be there to see me receive my degree. For that I was very thankful because without her tenacity, her reminders about getting an education, her understanding and encouragement and her sacrifices, this day may never have happened. It was a proud day for her and a small reward to a gracious and wonderful lady.

A PROUD AND HAPPY DAY FOR A WONDERFUL MOTHER

ROYAL VICTORIA HOSPITAL- UPPER CAMPUS

MY GOOD FRIEND ELLIOT YOUNG.
WE KNEW WE COULD DO IT!

'49 Students

David Rosen | **G. I. Piercey** | **P. L. White**

Mr. Rosen won the Lieutenant-Governor's Silver Medal in Health and Social Medicine and J. Francis Williams Scholarship in Medicine and Clinical Medicine; Mr. Piercey won the Robert Forsyth Prize in Surgery; Mr. White won the Campbell Howard Prize in Clinical Medicine.

Chapter VIII

Internship

Having finished with the graduation exercises it was time to leave Montreal which had been my adopted home for the past four years and I left with unforgettable memories of a tremendous experience. During my last year I had to make a decision of where I wanted to go to serve my internship. Before being granted a license to practice medicine it was mandatory that one had to spend a year in a hospital setting to gain some practical experience in caring for patients. Most of my class chose to stay in Montreal and spend their year in one of the several fine hospitals in that city. But I guess I had too much western blood in my veins because there never was any question as to where I wanted to go. I had made up my mind to be in Vancouver and I was accepted at the Vancouver General Hospital.

Doris and I had talked of this for some time and she was now in Vancouver having accepted a position at St. Paul's Hospital in their physiotherapy department in April. She had been unable to attend my graduation but our thoughts were on each other that day and were looking forward to being near each other again.

My Mother had had a very enjoyable time in Montreal. In addition to seeing me graduate she had met Doris' parents and family who were extremely hospitable and certainly made her welcome. I express my heartfelt thanks for that hospitality but also for the great kindness shown to me over the past couple of years. They were lovely people and I was sorry to be leaving them but I know they understood my desire to move westward.

So Mother and I started on our trip home. We spent a couple of days in Exeter, Ontario visiting my sister's husband's family whom she had not met. We had a brief stop at Niagara to view the falls on our way back to Toronto where we boarded the CN train for the homeward journey. It was so wonderful being together for those 4 days - relaxing and seeing the country and talking about so many different events of our past. It was a trip and a time that I will always cherish.

On our arrival in Vancouver we were met at the station by Doris and my sister, Zeta, who was now living in Vancouver where her husband was attending university. We spent a few days and then continued to Denman Island and my father. It was planned that after a few days Doris would join us on the Island in order to meet Dad and the rest of the clan. She was to take the ferry and then the bus to Buckley Bay where I would meet her. I had the idea that it would be more romantic if I went over there by row boat to bring her across the channel instead of crossing on the ferry - sort of like the idea of carrying your bride across the threshold of a new home. Doris got off the bus and looked lovely in all her finery of new clothes in preparation for the meeting of my family. I didn't tell her that it probably would have been more appropriate if she had worn hip waders because the boat leaked like a sieve. Doris sat in the rear bailing the boat with a can while I rowed. She still talks about my idea of a romantic sea cruise. My dad gave his stamp of approval so all ended well.

It was on that visit to Denman by Doris that I discovered she liked sea food. While growing up she had spent quite a number of summers with relatives in New Brunswick where she got to love clams, mussels and lobster. When she came to the Island she suggested that we go digging clams. Although I had grown up on the coast I had never tasted clams. I grew up in a home where we enjoyed salmon and cod and trout but had never eaten shell fish. My father had had a very severe allergic reaction after eating crabmeat and nearly died. To have an anaphylactic reaction on an isolated island was a serious, life threatening situation. So as a result of this we never had shell fish of any kind in our home.

So Doris and I went down to dig clams and at that time I discovered, to my surprise, that the shore line was covered with oysters. When I was growing up oysters were not seen on our shores. Just before the war some members of one of the many Japanese communities at Fanny Bay had imported some oysters from Japan and placed them at their logging wharfs for their own use. Well these oysters became accustomed to our waters and spawned and as a result the surrounding foreshores were just covered with small oysters, thus the beginning of a major, multimillion dollar industry in our area. So I not only tasted my first clams but also some oysters. My father sat and watched as we ate our enjoyable meal and I'm sure he expected us to "pip it" in very quick order.

This discovery of oysters growing on our shore was just one of the many changes that can occur within the short span of four years. The Japanese Canadians who brought these oysters over from Japan were no longer with us. Our expulsion of these people - most of whom had been born here - was a very sad commentary of just how our government treated some of our citizens of whom some were my friends. They were shipped like cattle to the interior of the Province at Salmo and Greenwood in the Kootenays, places which I was later to know very well, or to Alberta, without compensation. This was a very sad chapter in our Canadian history.

On my return to Vancouver I checked in at the Vancouver General Hospital and was alloted quite a nice suite in the internes quarters on Heather Street across the road from the hospital. I was fitted for my white uniforms that internes wore in those days and given a schedule of which wards I would be assigned to for the next few months. Junior internes were not too high in the pecking order of personnel around a hospital and certainly at the bottom of the heap when it came to remuneration. Our stipend was $25 each month plus our room and board and laundry. The excuse for this meagre pay scale was the argument that we were still receiving teaching and instructions in medicine. Fair enough. I can accept that. I was thankful that the years of paying for tuition and lodging and books and equipment were at an end because to me my debt load which I had amassed seemed to be looking more like a

Provincial or Federal debt. We soon learned that our time there was not all teaching and instruction as we were working some very long hours - both day and night - which some internes referred to as a "slave labor". However there is no use fighting tradition so just go along with the old saying - "Smile and wear beige".

My first rotation was to be a 2 month stay on the Paediatric floor dealing with sick children which was so different from dealing with adults. I was not there too long when the administrator asked me and 3 other internes to transfer to the infectious disease hospital. The reason for this was because of the Polio epidemic that was becoming a real concern in B.C.

Each day on an average, 15 or 20 patients were being sent into this hospital from all parts of the city and surrounding areas as suspects of having polio. One task was to first take a very detailed and careful history from each of them. Very little was known about the disease or why it occurred or how it was spread. We wanted to know where they had been, who were they with, had they been swimming, were they getting enough rest, what they had been eating and drinking etc etc. There were theories that swimming was a source because most outbreaks occurred in summer when it was hot. Other reasons were suspected such as being overtired and others suspected that it was acquired from certain foods such as chicken or from our drinking water. We did not know.

After taking a history we examined the patient and then began our investigation which included doing blood work and a spinal tap to obtain some fluid from the spinal canal to be checked for certain cells. From this we could determine if the patient indeed had polio or a virus infection that mimicked polio. Fortunately most of those people that we saw were released back to the community and their physician. Sadly however quite a number did prove to have the disease. They had to be isolated and observed. There was no cure. All that we could do was watch for the complications of the paralysis and try to protect the paralized muscles and limbs. If the muscles of the chest wall were involved it often became necessary to provide a respirator - referred to as the Iron Lung - to assist with their breathing.

This was a terrible epidemic to hit the province and left many people with varying disabilities. B.C. did experience another epidemic in 1954 when I was in practice in New Westminster. Shortly after this, thanks to Dr. Jonas Salk, we had Salk vaccine at our disposal and this great discovery has practically ended this debilitating disease.

We never did understand how and why these epidemics occurred. I do know that there were 4 junior internes that did not accept the view that getting overtired was a cause because after 2 months of being in close contact with these poor souls we were very tired and glad to get transferred to another ward. In addition to being beat it was a depressing place to work.

In the rest of our year we were back to our original rotation where we would spend a couple of months on each ward. after leaving the infectious disease hospital I went on the surgical wards where I assisted with operations and became involved in post operative care of the patient. In the maternity hospital we were involved with the delivery of babies and the postpartum care of mothers and babies until their time for discharge. On the medical wards we were involved with a great assortment of illnesses affecting people of all ages and of varying stages of their illness. Many, of course, were terminal cases.

I suppose our busiest rotation was when we were assigned to the Emergency Department. The internes were the primary care physicians for the great array of cases that arrived there. It was our job to assess every patient and give emergency treatment prior to referring them to their physician for follow up care or admitting them to hospital. No 2 shifts were ever the same and we would never know from one minute to the next just what the ambulance would bring us. This was a great training experience for an interne, many of whom would be going into practice in a short while.

There is a great deal more to medicine than what I have been describing as we went through medical school and our internship. One soon finds out that there is something not found in text books, not learned in the classroom, and not taught by our teachers. It is to do with the emotional understanding of this whole business. There are times of great joy and elation such as one sees in new parents after the birth of their child or the feeling of thanksgiving by a family member when a loved one is recovering from a serious illness or accident or when a patient learns that the pathology report on the lump you removed was benign. These are the times when the doctor is elated too.

Unfortunately, however there are also times when we must learn to deal with the grief and sadness and depression experienced by a patient when all has not gone well for themselves or for a loved one. We see this with serious illnesses and of course in terminal illnesses. These are the low points of our practice. There is no question that we as physicians become emotionally involved in our patients' affairs. We must do this in order to show compassion and understanding for the situation. In my view a physician that becomes so callous as not to be involved is never going to be a very respected individual. All of this is a very important part of medicine and must be experienced individually.

Just near the end of our year I had written some more exams set by the Medical Council of Canada. This body was recognized by all the provinces as the Council that would see that we were fit to be granted a license to practice. After the exams at McGill a year before these were quite easy ones to pass. I became a licentiate of the Medical Council of Canada and added four more letters after my name - L.M.C.C. I then went before the College of Physicians and Surgeons of B.C. and was granted my license.

During the spring I had a visit from my good friend, Elliott, who was interning in Boston. He was involved with a graduate nurse from Montreal who was living in Vancouver and this was his main reason for the trip. He informed me that he was continuing with his training and had been accepted for Pathology at Boston. We had a great few days of visit and I would be seeing him again shortly.

Doris was still at St. Paul's Hospital. We had made a decision to set a date to be married which would be on July 8th soon after I finished interning; so she decided to return to Montreal to spend some time with her parents and get ready for the big event.

The decision as to what to do the next year had been made. One possibility was to stay on at the hospital and enter into a residency program to train in one of the specialties. This I considered but really was unsure as to which specialty to take.

I felt I should enter general practice for a while to try to decide. I also felt that if I were going into general practice it should be out in the country away from the big centre. So after looking at a number of job opportunities, I decided to go to a place I had never seen. I was going to Fruitvale near Trail in the Kootenays of B.C.

I guess another pertinent factor in making the decision of what to do was that I was now 26. I was getting married. After seven long years of University I owed the Government Student Loan Program, my family and friends quite a substantial debt that had to be paid and finally I did not think that the stipend for internes would support me any longer.

CHAPTER IX

Kootenay Country

My year at the Vancouver General Hospital was over and time to say goodbye to my fellow internes who were going their different ways. The way for George Piercy was down to the C.P. station and my sixth train ride across Canada. My thoughts were not on what courses I would be taking or which professor I would meet. This trip was different. I was on my way to the altar and a life with a lovely girl I had met four years before at a basketball game.

The Sturgess home was a hive of activity in preparation for the wedding which was set for July 8, 1950. It was no place for me so I stayed with a relative of their family. My best friend, Elliott, had come up from Boston so we managed to keep busy. It seemed as if we had never been apart as we talked over our years together at McGill.

And then it all happened. Elliott was my best man and Doris' sister, Shirley, was bridesmaid. Doris looked lovely as she came up the aisle. After the wedding we had a very nice reception at the Ritz Carlton Hotel.

When it came time to reply to the toast to the bride my new wife gave me her first ultimatum. She told me in no uncertain terms not to say too much. So I became aware right from the start that she was going to play a role in any decision I was about to make.

I was happy that this important day was over and I was very thankful for a couple of reasons. I had arrived in Montreal with not much going for me but a dream and now I was about to leave with a degree in Medicine and a bride. The old town had been very good to me and I felt very well blessed.

We went up to the Laurentian Mountains to a place called Morin Heights for a short honeymoon. We stayed at a beautiful lodge on a lake that had just opened and we were made very welcome. We then spent a few days with Doris' parents before starting out on our trip. At this point in our life we were the proud owners of a new Pontiac. We motored to Niagara Falls and then crossed into the United States on our route to Chicago.

Our trip through Chicago was on a Sunday night and we found ourselves in an 8 lane highway that came to a point where it divided into a number of different directions. I was driving at the time and I spotted a green light which obviously was not the green light for my particular lane, nor was it the route the policeman on the corner wanted me to take. Across the intersection there was a squealing of brakes. I had created, probably, one of the worst traffic jams that the traffic policeman had ever seen and I'm sure there were cars backed up half the way up Lake Michigan. I can still see that policeman throwing his hat on the ground as he wondered how he was going to sort things out. He was one unhappy warrior and glad to see the last of this Canadian tourist. The rest of the trip across the northern states to Spokane was uneventful.

On our way through Minnesota we spent a couple of days in Rochester to visit the Mayo Clinic. A fraternity brother of mine was doing a residency in surgery. It was an eye opener to see the methods they had of seeing the large number of patients that arrived there daily.

Patients were not necessarily admitted to a hospital but would be registered in various hotels and motels and boarding homes located in Rochester. Even some of their post operative care was conducted in these quarters.

Investigation of these serious and complicated cases that had been referred to the clinic were conducted by very competent and trained teams of specialists, and some carefully chosen bright young residents and internes. Patients were from all across the mid-western states and central Canada. The operative slates were in full swing both day and night. With my fraternity brother, Tony, I was able to observe some of the surgery being done during our two days stay there - quite mind boggling cases. It certainly was an eye opener of what could be accomplished in a large clinic such as this world famous Mayo Clinic which had been started by a pair of brothers practicing in this area and who had a dream.

At Spokane we drove north to cross the border on our way to Trail. About the only thing I knew about Trail was that it was the home of the Trail Smokeaters of hockey fame. It was a city of 15,000 people where the Consolidated Mining and Smelting Company had its huge plant for extracting the metals from the ore that was mined in Kimberly B.C. at the Sullivan Mine. The two main metals produced were lead and zinc but there was also gold and silver. The fumes from the smelter contained a number of harmful materials, some of which ended up as sulphuric acid which had a devastating effect on the environment. There was no vegetation on the hills around Trail and this desolation extended down the Columbia River basin well into the United States. Steps were being taken to reduce these harmful emissions and by using these chemicals they had established a very large and lucrative chemical fertilizer industry. When we arrived there were the first signs that a bit of vegetation was beginning to appear on the hillside. But it was still a desolate looking place and Doris and I were not impressed. To take your bride to this setting was a real test of one's marriage.

I had contracted to work at the C.S. Williams clinic. It was a well known clinic and served as a referral centre for the West Kootenays. When I started there were 24 doctors on this roster. They maintained a number of satellite offices in the surrounding area. A long established one was in Rossland, another at Castlegar and they had one in Fruitvale where I was to work and also live there becoming their first resident doctor.

The origin of Trail stems from the mining discoveries that were happening all over the west and east Kootenays and extending also south of the border in Idaho, Montana and the Spokane area. Rossland - just four miles from Trail - was the site of an early gold discovery and the creation of a mine to extract ore from this large deposit followed. Because of all this activity it was necessary to build a smelter for the processing of this ore. Trail was chosen as the site and probably the main reason for this was a source of hydroelectric power that could be generated on the Columbia River that ran through the area. This mighty river proved to be very important in the future of the smelter as it grew to become one of the leading smelters in the world.

We arrived in Trail about noon in the third week of July. I'm sure the temperature was about 105 in the shade which didn't improve our feelings toward this part of the world. We stopped at the clinic and after introducing ourselves we proceeded out to the Beaver Valley where Fruitvale was located. It was in sharp contrast to Trail. There was a small river in the valley and everything was very green and lush and seemed very pleasant. There was a small village with a few stores and a small hotel. A railroad ran through the area. Across the tracks on a hill was the house that the clinic had purchased and where we would live. It certainly was a more desirable setting than in beside the smelter.

It took a few days to get settled and round up enough furniture for our first home. I did not carry Doris across the threshold when we moved into the house. My failed attempt at being romantic when I rowed her across to Denman had left an impression on my mind.

On our first night in the house there was a sudden and loud pounding on our door at about eleven o'clock - we still did not have a phone. The residents had heard that the new doctor had moved in and he was wanted urgently at the local cafe which was a couple of hundred yards away. I certainly was not ready to start making calls as I didn't even have a medical bag. I quickly went down to see what the problem was and learned that the owner of the cafe was lying on the floor behind the counter in a semiconscious state and her colour was not that rosy. I was able to tear a piece of tubing off the beer dispensing machine next door and get it inserted down her throat to create an airway and this certainly improved her colour and condition and possibly played a part in saving her life.

When the real story was obtained, she had bent down beside a cooler to unplug it for some reason and her earring touched a water pipe that ran up the inside of the wall. She had electrocuted herself. She had burns to the side of her face and within a few days, after admission to hospital, it became clear that she was going to lose her ear.

The cafe where all this occurred was in the hotel and adjoining the local beer parlour and it was about the time the local patrons were thinking of leaving. It was quite obvious that a fair number had had a few too many. Everyone there was watching every move the new doctor was making.

I tell this story because when one starts out in practice it is most important to try and establish a good record and reputation. I'm quite sure that nearly everyone in the valley quickly learned how Fruitvale's first resident physician had saved this poor lady's life and I'm also sure that they heard it by listening to a dozen different interpretations of just what had happened that night. I certainly didn't have to advertise.

About twenty five years later when I was practising in New Westminster I went into one of my examining rooms and didn't recognize the patient until I saw that she only had one ear. She was visiting and heard I was there and had just dropped in to thank me again. An event like this is impressive to a doctor and brings home the fact that some do appreciate our efforts.

Getting settled in our first home was interesting. To complicate matters we inherited a dog with the house. He had refused to leave with the previous owners. We learned from the neighbours that his name was Andy. At some time in his life he got mixed up with a trap but got along quite well with only three legs. There never was a dull moment with Andy.

On our first weekend in the house Doris had bought a couple of steaks that we were going to have for Sunday dinner. As we had no refrigerator the steaks were stored in the basement which was the coolest place in the house. Andy obviously felt they were for him because when we went to get them all we could find was some brown butcher's paper.

He became, for some reason, very protective of me. One evening when we were having our dinner I heard this terrible todo outside my back porch and as I looked out Andy had a man treed about five feet up a weeping willow. The man, I learned, was just coming to see if I could do anything for his toothache.

In a way I became attached to this Heinz but the day came when I had to find a new owner for him. He learned where my office was and in spite of my efforts to keep him at home he became a frequent visitor at my office door and didn't always take a friendly approach to some of my patients. The final straw came when he grabbed a lady's purse and pulled her down to the pavement. In grabbing that purse I think he was aware that quite a number of patients did not pay their doctor's fees in those days.

We were becoming citizens of this rural community. Doris

went to work as a physiotherapist at the Trail Hospital. I was involved in my first practice and getting busier. When I contracted to work at the C.S. Williams Clinic I was to work in the Clinic in Trail in the morning and in my office in Fruitvale in the afternoon. I was also on staff at the hospital. Gradually we were getting to know a few people in the area and enjoying their company as we socialized.

My work was always interesting and variable. In my office which I inherited there were some forceps for pulling teeth and I did a few extractions. I knew nothing about the technique of anaesthetizing a tooth but got by by giving the patient a shot of morphine which worked very well.

A number of times I was called upon to act as a veterinarian. I had a number of dogs brought to my office that had got mixed up with a porcupine. Prior to removing the quills I gave the poor animal a few whiffs of chloroform. I later learned that chloroform can be quite lethal to dogs but I guess I was just lucky. On one occasion I was asked to see a dog that had been hit by a car and had sustained a major laceration over its hip and back. I painstakingly sutured this wound only to learn that the dog had removed all of my sutures by the next day. In spite of my efforts the wound healed quite well. Nature is a wonderful healer.

There was no veterinarian in the area and quite a few farmers came to me to get penicillin for their cattle for various problems. They knew more about these conditions and the treatment than I did.

Not too far from where we lived a farmer was demolishing an old barn. I approached him about getting enough lumber to build a carport. I worked like a beaver constructing what I thought was a pretty fine looking structure. No one told me about the snowfall that this part of the world had because I built it at the back of the lot about 150 feet from the road. The first snow came on Nov. 11. I remember the date very well because I had to shovel out my driveway to go into Trail to attend a patient who was remembering the war and attending a members day at the Legion. After leaving, his car failed to make a turn in the road and he was badly injured. When I returned home later in the day I just parked my car on the street hoping to reshovel the driveway the next morning. Well, I never got to use that carport again till next spring. I had never seen so much snow in my life. At least the carport withstood the snowpack.

The first winter there was a cold one. We heated the house with a sawdust burner. For those who are not familiar with this method, the furnace had a large hopper on the side which held several large buckets of sawdust which trickled into the burner. This was a common form of heating on the coast and it worked well but in the colder climates quite often the sawdust became frozen, especially when one had to get another truck load from the mill in the middle of winter. Keeping this furnace stoked was often a full time job.

So we were happy to welcome spring. In June Doris gave birth to our first child - a lovely little girl whom we named Janet. We had more to occupy our minds now than just coping with Andy.

Summer in the Kootenay region was very pleasant. There were some large lakes nearby that we visited quite often. We planted a large garden and had so much produce that we had to rent a locker in the cold storage outlet. The hot summers in this part of the world were great for growing vegetables.

The west Kootenay area was the centre of the Doukhobor community in B.C.. These people had emigrated from Russia in the early part of the century and settled in the surrounding country side becoming a very progressive group. They lived in communal groupings. Many years earlier they had built an irrigation system that extended for miles turning their large tracts of land into a very productive area. They became quite an affluent group and branched out into the community in various trades and businesses and some became prominent community leaders. Their communal living has almost died out.

Quite a number became my patients and some became good friends. We certainly enjoyed visiting with them and learning their customs. While in New Westminster one of them, Virginia, lived with us for the better part of a year. We became very fond of this lovely young lady.

The great majority of them were what was known as Orthodox Doukhobors. We also had to deal with a small minority known as the Sons of Freedom. These "Freedomites" did strange things to get attention and promote their cause. I never did learn or understand what that cause was or just what they wanted. They would parade around in the nude in public, they would burn their own homes and occasionally they would blow up a power line. Fortunately they were in the minority and did not alter my opinion of the fine people that formed the majority.

My work kept me busy and my practice was getting larger. I was doing quite a bit in obstetrics and it was at this time that the Clinic approached me about going back in a residency program at the Vancouver General to become certified in this field. They were prepared to underwrite the cost of my training with one stipulation of course and that was I was to return to Trail on completion. This gave me a lot to think about and I was not about to rush into this proposal.

At the Clinic we, of course, were involved in Industrial Medicine. They had a contract with the Smelting Company to periodically assess their workers for a number of conditions - the main one being lead poisoning. From the appearance of the blood cells we could determine if a worker was being over exposed to lead. If so, the worker had to be placed in a different part of the smelter until the signs had disappeared. This was a common, serious problem.

The company was one of the first to provide a comprehensive health care plan for their employees. Apart from this group, most people had no form of prepaid medical plan. Those practicing in the rural areas did receive a lot of vegetables, fruit, eggs, chickens, etc. in payment of their account.

We were still pondering our future. In spite of the good friends we had got to know in the area, we were not particularily happy about spending the rest of our life here. So at Easter of our second year we took a trip to the Coast as I was having second thoughts about moving to Vancouver Island and on this trip visited a couple of locations where there were openings for another physician. In May a friend of mine, Adam Waldie, who had practiced in Castlegar phoned me to tell me about a practice in New Westminster where the owner - a classmate of Adam's - had become quite ill and needed some help. So we decided, after a quick trip to meet this doctor, to make the move and I gave my notice to the Clinic that I would be leaving at the end of June.

I have never had any regrets about having spent this time in the Kootenays. I got to see and learn about this very interesting and historic part of our province. I gained a great deal of experience and the doctors at the Clinic were very good to me. It was a wonderful working environment for a young fellow starting his first practice. So for a number of reasons I was sorry to go, but we had made our decision.

CHAPTER X

The Royal City

Happily we were back on the West Coast where we were to begin a new phase of our life. No long term commitment had been made as I began working with Dr. Gordon Mathias in New Westminster. Little did we know that I would spend the next 23 years in this office.

Gordon was a few years older than I was. He had been on staff at the University of B.C. teaching bacteriology but decided to leave that post and enter medical school in Edmonton. After graduation he opened an office in the West End of New Westminster in 1946 and by the time I joined him he had a very large practice. Because of his health he no longer could continue on his own and needed some assistance. He suffered from asthma and quite often was confined to bed because of lung infections.

We soon became very good friends and we worked well together. I admired his dedication and his understanding of his patients. He was a very kind and compassionate person and in my eyes he had all the qualities that were necessary to becoming a good and respected physician. He certainly was respected in his community and it was my hope to emulate this man.

After about a year together he approached me and offered me a partnership in his practice. By this time Doris and I were getting to know the area and felt that we could be quite happy to settle here. So I accepted his offer and looked foward to a long association with him.

This, however, was not to happen. Within a year Gordon, to everyone's sorrow, suddenly died from pneumonia and a massive lung abscess. He was just 41 years of age and left a wife and three young children. I accepted this tragedy as if it were a member of my own family. His wife and I discussed the situation in relation to the office and the practice and she asked me if I were interested in purchasing his share. I knew that, of course, would settle any question of where we were going to make our home. I agreed with the terms of the sale and this is how my medical future was finalized.

New Westminster was once called Queensborough. The Governor of the colony and some of the leading citizens of the area were having thoughts and arguments about changing the name and finally the Colonial Secretary wrote to Queen Victoria asking "as a special mark of Royal favour" if she would name the city. A letter was received in 1859 from the Secretary of State that read, "I am commanded to acquaint you that Her Majesty has been graciously pleased to decide that the capital of British Columbia shall be called New Westminster".

On July 20, 1859 Governor Douglas issued a proclamation announcing the change from Queensborough. So this is how it got the name "The Royal City". In 1868, however, the government offices were moved to Victoria and that is another story that caused a great deal of debate.

When we arrived here in 1952 it was a city with a population of about 30,000. It was primarily an industrial city with a number of large mills and manufacturing plants along the Fraser River. It was a major shipping point with its deep sea piers and facilities. Across the Patullo Bridge lay Surrey and the vast rural area of the Fraser Valley and New Westminster was the supply and commercial centre that served this area.

Making this an ideal location in which to get established and to raise a family was the fact that the city had good schools, a good transportation system within the city and with Vancouver, hundreds of acres of parkland and good recreational and athletic facilities and all the amenities for shopping. There was a very wonderful community spirit in the city with pride in it's past and a good outlook for it's future. It was a city that was exciting and alive.

It also had two very fine hospitals within its boundaries - the Royal Columbian Hospital and St. Mary's. The Columbian had a large nursing school attached and it also was a teaching hospital for training of internes. I became an active Staff member of both hospitals and enjoyed my many years of practice in them with full privileges.

In a very short time I realized that the work load of this busy and growing practice was becoming too much for one person and I began looking for an associate. One of the internes who was just finishing his term at the Columbian

Hospital was Jack Wright. He was a well qualified graduate from Toronto. We began our practice together in 1954 and continued until I left New Westminster in 1974. It was a happy and remarkable relationship that we enjoyed. Our families became close friends and it was with sadness that he passed away in 1997. We still visit and holiday with his wife, Dorothy who now lives in Duncan on Vancouver Island.

Our office was located at the corner of 8th Ave. and 20th Street in the west end of New Westminster, about 2 blocks from the Fraser River and where Marine Drive enters the city. The office building was built in 1947 by Gordon Mathias and contained dental suites, a large pharmacy and four apartments above. Doris and I lived here in one of those suites when we first moved from the Kootenays.

The West End was an established middle class area lying to the west of Kingsway. Our practice was not confined to this area alone. I often tell people that we, not infrequently, made calls to our patients across the Patullo Bridge in Surrey. At that time there were only four doctors with offices in this vast area between the bridge and the U.S. Border. What a change. Today Surrey is one of the largest municipalities in the province, both in area and population. We abutted Burnaby and while we practiced at this location they built the Queensborough Bridge, from Lulu Island and Queensborough, that ended at the foot of 20th Street- a few blocks from our office.

Jack and I covered for each other in the evenings and on weekends. Both of us had a large maternity practice and we got to know each others maternity patients in case one of us was not available.

In the fifties and before, generalists practiced in isolation, not sharing their practice with other doctors. They tended to be on call 24 hours a day and seven days a week. The reason for this was strange to me. Perhaps that work ethic stemmed from the depression years when times were not that great for practitioners and they may have worried about losing a patient to a competitor, or it may have been an egotistical attitude that no one could take care of their patients as they could. In any event it was quite a sad attitude.

We had a very different view which was quite a revolutionary idea of how we should work together. We formed a partnership-not an associate arrangement as some had in those days where they might share an office. Everything was shared. We alternated our nights on call and our weekends. We made rounds in the hospital together, seeing each others patients and getting to know them. Some of our colleagues expressed doubt as to whether this would be accepted by the people under our care. But they knew of the arrangement and did accept it and were very happy with the system. When they called for an appointment they did not seem to mind which doctor would be seeing them. We shared our expenses and our remuneration on an equal basis. It was a true partnership in every sense of the word. In this way we had our time off for relaxation and rest which is so important.

I can recall at one busy time while making rounds I asked a patient that I had delivered a few days before if she would like to have her baby circumcised. She informed me that it would not be necessary. When I went to examine the baby before discharge, to my surprise and embarrassment, it was a girl. This is a mental error that can occur when one gets too busy.

St. Mary's Hospital had just moved to their new facility and the press were there for the opening ceremonies. They learned that I had delivered the first baby in the new wing and that I had also delivered the last one in the old hospital. This story appeared in the local paper. I had a call that night from a lady that informed me that she was about to have twins and wondered if I would deliver one in the old hospital and one in the new one, and she sounded serious. It took me a few minutes but I finally recognized the voice. It was my partner's wife, Dottie, giving me a bad time and having some fun.

For most of our years together we did a fair amount of surgery. We had an ideal working arrangement and worked as partners helping each other. We were both busy on the hospital active staff and spent a lot of time at committee meetings to deal with the operation of the hospitals. To put it plainly, we were both very busy with a large general practice.

Our surgery was done at both the local hospitals but that done at the Royal Columbian Hospital stands out in my memory, mainly because of the head nurse of the operating theatres named Miss Doherty. She was a person who believed in going by the book to the letter. When she stated the time to start your operation was 7:00 a.m. she did not mean 7:01. One would have thought she had trained in England where the nursing sisters ruled with an iron fist. Her office was immediately next to the elevators that were used to get to the O.R. on the fifth floor. As you got off the elevator the first person to see was always Miss Doherty. This buxom person would be standing with her arms folded across her chest and mornings were not the time of day for her to smile. If you were late the greeting was always the same-"Doctor, you're late".

She was a very formidable obstacle to try and get past in order to get to the doctors' change room some 50 feet down the corridor and the tirade would begin immediately and by the time you managed to get there you felt about 3 inches tall. On quite a number of occasions I would run up the stairway at the other end of the corridor rather than face her as I got off the elevator.

For the rest of the day she reverted to quite a normal person. Not infrequently, when I was to scrub for an operation, I would remove my wedding band and put it in a pocket of my operating gown. Sometimes after surgery I would forget to put it back on my finger. Usually, late in the day, I would discover this and phone her desk to see if they could find it before going off to the laundry. She always managed to find it and gave me a call so she certainly wasn't always difficult to get along with. But occasionaly I dream that I have slept in and must face Miss Doherty as I get off that elevator.

Getting along with staff at the hospital was never too difficult a task for me but I must relate an episode that occurred one morning as I was entering one of the wards to make my rounds. Just as I entered the ward one of the nurses was bending over a fairly deep laundry bin looking for something that had been inadvertently put there by mistake. Anyway, pretty well all I could see was the bin and her rear end as she bent over. Without thinking, the temptation was too great and I gave her a fairly good swak as I walked by with my stethoscope that I was swinging beside me as I walked along. I am very thankful that my reflexes were pretty good in those days because the rest of her emerged from that bin at the speed of lightning. Both arms were swinging as if she were a karate expert and I'm sure to this day, if she had connected, I would have been out cold. Every once in a while one gets a sudden impulse and does some crazy thing on the spur of the moment.

Our first home that we bought was a small bungalow at 1927 London Street and not too far from my office. Soon after moving into it we had a surprise visit from our good friend, Elliott Young. He had just arrived in the San Francisco area on his return from almost 2 years in the Korean War where he served as a medical officer in a M.A.S.H. unit. It was extremely interesting to learn what a medical officer did in the hills of Korea in wartime. He took a quick trip up to New Westminster for a few days. He was certainly glad to get back on American soil again. He flew back to Boston to his wife, Viccy, and his infant son who was born shortly after he left for the war and whom he had not seen except in pictures.

So we were both now involved with a young family and ours was about to increase. While living at 1927 London Street our second daughter, Sharon, was born. I jokingly told most of my friends that we were going to have a boy and that I would call him "Charlie". Well this new baby was not a boy but the name "Charlie" has stuck to my daughter Sharon ever since. Later our son, George, was born and it became patently clear that with our new family it was necessary to have a bigger home. So we bought 1808 Edinburgh Street about 2 blocks from where we lived.

This home on Edinburgh Street was a beautiful two story colonial structure. The extra space was certainly welcome after our cramped quarters on London Street.

While here, quite a serious accident occurred which we both remember. One morning, on the way to the hospital, I called at the home of some friends to see their son who was quite ill.

During my conversation with the husband I mentioned that my day had not started that well as I woke up to a leaking roof over my bedroom. He was a millwright at one of the mills in town and he offered to have a look at it because it was his day off. I thanked him for his kind offer and proceeded to the hospital. Not too long after that I was paged on the intercom that I was needed in the emergency room. When I answered the call I was shocked to see my friend, Guy Titley, who had offered to look at our leaky roof. He had looked at it, alright. While up on the wet roof he slipped and fell 2 stories onto our front lawn which brought a passerby to the door who asked Doris if she knew there was a man lying on her lawn. After my examination and investigation I learned that this man had fractured his back, his arm and three ribs. He kept apologizing because he knew he had upset my wife. He did make a very complete recovery in due course. I will never forget his kind offer made that wet morning.

My three children gave me a great deal of pleasure and I look upon their "growing up" years as probably the happiest and most fulfilling years of my life. As is the case with most parents we became involved in all of their activities, their school work and their friends.

On a couple of occasions when they were small we took them to Montreal to visit their grandparents and for the grandparents to assess them. And of course we travelled by train. After my first trip across Canada to enter medical school, which I enjoyed very much, I was never too thrilled about spending four or five days vibrating back and forth. In fact, I detested such trips and I had already made six such excursions. However it is no secret that everyone knew that I was petrified about flying. It stems from my acrophobia or fear of heights which I had always had. I can recall my father taking me up to the highest point on Denman to show me the new fire lookout tower that was about 100 feet tall. He started up the open stairs expecting me to follow. When I was about 10 feet off the ground I froze and had to be helped down. This was difficult for my dad to understand as he had no fear of heights. Even today I cannot go out on an open balcony if it is more than two stories high. So this explains our trips across the country by train.

It was not until 1964 when I finally talked myself into a plane ride when we all went to Hawaii at the Easter break. When I suggested going, Doris asked me if it would be by boat. To her great surprise and shock, I said that "Oh no, we will fly". She loves flying and never could understand anyone who would travel any other way. I just thought that the flight was the greatest and since then have done quite a bit of flying and enjoy it. I still cannot walk out on an open balcony which to me is very strange and I know others who experience the same feeling.

Our family vacations together were always events that I really looked forward to doing. I often regret that we did not take more. When you are busy and working hard sometimes one tends to delay these happy times or not see their importance at the time. I think in my case, occasionally perhaps, I felt the necessity to be attending to the practice and that I had to be present for certain cases. One finally realizes that this is the wrong philosophy and learns that the world will not fall apart if one is not on the job. I guess it's a type of ego trip to think that others may not be capable of taking your place.

And we were happy about being back on the Coast because we were able to visit my parents on the Island in spite of the ferry rides and waiting in lineups. Both were getting older and

I was happy that my children were getting to know them. Both of my grandfathers and one grandmother were dead when I was a child and I often wish that I had known them. We enjoyed these visits to the Island and the Comox Valley so much that I purchased some beach property on Denman Island and proceeded to build a small vacation home there.

As a young doctor I was exposed to the work of the Kinsmen Club of New Westminster. Kinsmen clubs were started in Canada and were service clubs for young men under 40 years of age only. I had experienced 2 major polio epidemics in B.C. - one while interning and again in 1954 when I was in private practice. I admired the dedication of the Kinsmen in their service club work regarding this disease. Firstly their work in raising funds for research through the Mothers' March campaigns and then in the program in which they were involved in helping those that suffered permanent injury. They provided funds for the purchase of page turners that would turn the pages of a book by touching a button by their chin - a wonderful invention for those that had paralysis of their arms. And there was the program of building ramps and elevator lifts for those in wheel chairs. This spirit of helping others in the community and giving of their time so freely impressed me and I joined the club. Over the years we became involved in other projects besides the polio activities. I can remember the hours that we all spent in converting the old machine shop on the grounds of Trapp Tech High School, which had just been demolished, into a school and an activity centre for handicapped children. The friendship that develops among club members on these projects and at our weekly dinner meetings was so important in establishing relationships that still exist. Doris joined the Kinette club and became an active member as well.

I had always had an interest in sports and especially baseball. When my son reached the age for team play I took him to Queen's Park Arena where they were conducting registrations. They were very adamant that they had to play within very definite age parameters. When they asked the date of his birth he looked up at me and I looked down at him. Neither of us could remember the date - just one of life's very embarrassing moments. George became a very good player and when he entered Babe Ruth League he was on the New Westminster all star team in the Provincial finals.

I became involved with the organization and served as president of the Babe Ruth League as well as serving on the Provincial Amateur Baseball Association for one year. Many hours were spent at the edge of a baseball diamond as he grew up. Doris became an official score keeper and was one of the best at that job - recording all the plays and hits and errors in each game.

It was always my ambition to plan and build a home. I guess I got tired of people saying "Oh, you live in so and so's house". Well it was not so and so's house because I had bought and owned it and it was mine. I had bought a lot in Massey Heights, a new development in the city and located on what once was, when we moved to town, a goat farm. We built our home at 912 Jackson Crescent and lived there for the rest of our time in New Westminster.

The time arrived when I was wondering about my future as the years of a busy and hectic practice were causing concerns. I had experienced a couple of health problems and I was losing some of the old energy that I had when I started into this business after graduating nearly 25 years before. No longer could I get up after being out for half of the night on call and shake my head under a cold water tap and be ready to start a full day. So I knew I would have to do something.

A great number of my patients had been with me since I started out and many were of my age and I knew them very well. To try and cut down on one's practice is a very difficult matter. One can't say to a patient that I will not be caring for you any longer and saying to the next one that I will continue to be your doctor. As well, the nature of my practice was changing. Because of their aging their health problems were changing. The years were flying by too quickly and nothing brought this home to me as forcibly as the fact that I was now seeing quite a number of young ladies coming to me as maternity patients and knowing that I had been present to bring them into the world. I had watched them progress from infants in the nursery through their development years into adult life. All of this certainly doesn't make one feel any younger but I had 25 wonderful years.

It had always been on our mind that sometime we would move over to the quieter life on the Island and this was one of the reasons for buying property over there. We were now spending more and more time at our vacation home and when we were returning to the lower mainland and getting off the ferry we, quite often, asked each other "Why are we coming back".

Our family was growing up. Janet was married and "Charlie" was planning to do the same. George was still at home but that would not be for many years. Doris and I were thinking of the time we would be alone again as “empty nesters”.

Other things were changing. My Father, at age 83, had passed away and the man whom I respected and loved was gone and I missed him. My Mother continued to live in the family home on the ranch.

So we pretty well had made up our minds that we would move. Jack Wright, my partner, was going to continue at the office and a young pair of doctors - husband and wife - were interested in buying my practice. I was only 50 and I knew that I would have to find something else to do. One option was to do locums i.e. relieving other doctors when they were on holiday but one thing I knew that I was going to do and that was nothing for a year. I was going fishing.

So everthing seemed to fall smoothly into place. We sold our Jackson Crescent home, I demitted from the hospital staffs, Dr. Jack was going to stay at the office, Drs. Tom and Chris Thomson became Dr. George, I received an honorary life membership in the Westminster Medical Society, we found a home in Comox and we left the Royal City.

The Royal City had been a great place to practice and live and raise a family. All of my family look back on those years with very life long and fond memories. I could go on writing many stories about events in our family life, of cases I saw in practice, of the many people we met and befriended. But this is life. Change in one’s surroundings and outlook and plans do change and we can only trust that all will work out happily in the end.

JANET, "CHARLIE" AND GEORGE

1808 EDINBURGH STREET

The BRITISH COLUMBIAN

NEW WESTMINSTER, B.C. 5 Cents Monday, Nov. 10, 1958

—Columbian photo by Sheamus Smith

THESE TWO BABIES share history in New Westminster. Mrs. Jane Fiebler, 140 East Sixteenth avenue, Burnaby, shows off her baby Derek Shawn, first-born in the new St. Mary's hospital. Mrs. Iris Wilkes, 572 Colby street, New Westminster, holds her baby, Susan Marie, last baby born in the old building of St. Mary's. In center is Dr. G. Piercy who delivered both "historic" babies.

RETIREMENT PARTY- 1974
MY STAFF LOOK HAPPY TO SEE ME GO!

WITH MY PARTNER AND FRIEND JACK WRIGHT

Chapter XI

Back Home

Comox is situated on a peninsula and is one of the few municipalities on Vancouver Island that faces a body of water looking back towards the Island. It's history goes back to the time of the earliest settlers who arrived by sailing ships at this port. The British Admiralty had holdings here and on this property at thc present time there is a navy cadet camp where hundreds and hundreds of young sailors from all across Canada spend part of their summer. During the second world war there was a naval training base at the same location. Comox also has a long association with the Canadian Air Force. Except for a few years after the war, when it was closed, it has been an active air base. C.F.B. Comox, at the time we moved here, was home to four squadrons and had a very significant role in the defense of our nation and in the economy of the region. Since then the fighter squadron has moved to Cold Lake but the base remains the only air base on the Pacific Coast.

Comox was once called Port Augusta. For reasons unknown to me the name was changed to Comox. I have heard of several words which were the origin of the name - Komoux and also Komas. The word Komoux is a native word meaning "land of plenty". Regardless of the origin of the name or the reasons for the name change, it is now called Comox. In my view it is well named as I do consider this a "land of plenty".

In January 1974 we moved to Comox where I had gone to school and left in 1942. In the previous fall we had been negotiating the purchase of a home that the builder was building for his wife. After several trips I think he got tired of me bugging him into selling. I still see his wife occasionally and she always says "you stole my home". I guess we did and she was not too happy with her builder husband-but the Piercys were very pleased.

The first year was a time of relaxation and not doing a great deal to justify my existence. I did put in a lawn and did some landscaping. We bought a boat which seemed to be the thing to do in a town with a large marina and as the summer progressed Doris and I became pretty good fisherpersons. We also managed a couple of overnight boating trips including one to Desolation Sound on the mainland.

George moved in with us in June as he had remained in New Westminster to complete his year in High School. Sharon had married and was living in Courtenay a few kilometers away and Janet remained on the mainland and was living in

Surrey and raising a family.

Toward the end of our first year in town I began to have thoughts about getting back into medicine in some way. After 25 years it gets in one's blood and I missed meeting and seeing patients. Besides my batteries were becoming charged again after a very relaxing year.

So I started doing locums - working in other doctor's offices when they were away. There was a great demand for this type of work as it is often impossible to find a replacement and I had experienced this situation on a number of occasions in my own practice. I certainly did not enjoy this type of work. I really never got to know the patients and there was no real follow up because quite often the patient's regular doctor returned before results were obtained. Besides that, it is too easy to develop bad habits of doing something or nothing on a temporary basis knowing that the other doctor would soon be back. So I was not a particularily happy warrior. It just wasn't my type of practice.

One of the physicians that I was relieving advised me that he was considering moving to California and wondered if I would be interested in buying into the Comox Medical Clinic where he was associated with 4 other doctors. I decided that I would accept his offer but I would limit my practice mainly to an office practice. I had had enough of being on call for emergency wards and delivering babies at all hours of the day and night and I had no intention of building up a sizeable practice again. So I was about to again be involved with the career that I loved and looked forward to working with my new associates at the Comox Clinic. I was about to spend 15 years there.

Soon after moving to Comox I joined the Comox Rotary

Club and became involved with service club work again. I felt good about the time that I was a Kinsman. I think the presence of service clubs in a community is a pretty good barometer of the health, the spirit and the vitality of that community and their work is so worthwhile.

The Comox Rotary was a young, active club and prior to my joining them they had built the d'Esterre House - an activity centre for seniors and for this effort they had received an international award. They have been involved in quite a number of major projects in town since then.

Fund raising is always a challenge for service clubs. I can recall when the club decided to cut and split wood as a fund raiser. One of the members knew a person who owned a fairly large lot in a subdivision and wanted it cleared so he could build a home. We certainly were willing to take on this source of wood supply. Sadly, at our next dinner meeting, we were appraised of the fact that we had cleared the wrong lot! We were fortunate to be able to negotiate our way out of this serious error.

One evening at a cocktail party we met the administrator of the Cumberland Hospital. When he learned that Doris was a Physiotherapist he immediately offered her a job to fill a vacancy on a temporary basis until the regular physio returned. Doris was hesitant as she had not worked at this since we lived in Trail some 25 years ago. After giving it a lot of thought she rejoined the C.P.A., borrowed books from the Toronto library, studied again and accepted the offer to start work in August of that year. It was for one half day each day and that suited Doris. Well, this temporary job lasted for 19 years. She built the department into a modern unit with new equipment and was the department head for all those years. She has fond memories of Cumberland.

So we were both becoming involved in our new community. Doris joined the Soroptimist Club in Courtenay which was a business and professional women's service club and she served as president of that organization for two consecutive years. I became a director of the Bevan Lodge Society that administered Bevan Lodge - a residence for mentally handicapped young people. But in spite of Doris' new job, my work at the clinic and our involvement with the community organizations, we were enjoying our new life in Comox. We had time for our boating and fishing and I got back to playing golf again and we were able to take some trips together. Life in the slow lane was great.

It was during my second year in town that I made a decision that opened up a new career for me. I had always been interested in politics. I may have inherited that desire from my grandfather Ballson who was so involved with the formation of municipal government status for the city of Vancouver. Quite often I would wander over to the town hall on council nights and listen to the deliberations of the Mayor and aldermen. I expressed some interest in this to a couple of my friends who encouraged me to run for office. I couldn't resist.

In the meantime I became a director on the Board of Glacier View Lodge which is a community owned care facility and home to 100 elderly residents. I served on this board for 9 years and served as the chairman for the last 3 years. Since leaving there the Lodge has been in the headlines of the paper because of their firm stand against the government's legislation to expropriate this private property without compensation. The

N.D.P. (Naive Dishonest Party) government has backed off on their ill conceived thinking but the legislation is still on the books in Victoria. Justice Mary Southin of the B.C. Court of Appeal suggested that the law should be repealed and urged the government to do so. However no action has been taken. It probably won't be removed until after the next election. The expropriation of private property without compensation is so against all decency that I trust it will never occur in this land.

I took a demit from the Rotary Club because I had joined the Shriners. A lot of people look upon our organization as a bunch of fellows wearing funny costumes, or riding go-carts in parades or marching to the tune of crazy oriental bands, or acting as clowns and having a lot of fun. Well we certainly do have some crazy fun times together but it should be pointed out that we belong to North America's greatest philanthropy that owns and operates 23 hospitals devoted to the care of crippled and burned children at no cost to the family or help from any government. We are all dedicated to working amd contributing to this great charity. Our wives, the Daughters of the Nile, also support this cause and Doris is a member. I am actively involved and have been a Medical Director for the Shrine of B.C. and the Yukon for the past 10 years.

When we left the Royal City some of our friends questioned the wisdom of such a move after spending so many years over there. We were aware of the problems that sometimes are experienced by people who move and try to become established in a new environment. We certainly have no regrets about the move. We do miss our circle of New Westminster friends but we have met so many people that have become our new friends and we find our life very fulfilling.

Comox has become our adopted city of which we are very proud.

MOTHER AND DAD - 40TH ANNIVERSARY

MY CLAN. GEORGE HASN'T LEARNED TO SMILE YET!

CHAPTER XII

Municipal Affairs

Time for the civic election of Dec. 1975 rolled around and I filed my nomination papers for the position of alderman. Campaigning certainly didn't turn me on. Knocking on doors and speaking at candidate meetings made me feel like a prostitute trying to sell myself and in all future elections I felt the same way. I detested this but I guess it is necessary and in my case it paid off as I easily won over the other 7 candidates. At the next election I ran for the office of Mayor and was elected.

I was successful in every one of my 9 campaigns and served on Comox Council for 19 years and as Mayor for the majority of that time.

Socrates, in 293 B.C. wrote "No man enters a trade for

which he is not qualified. But everyone believes they are qualified for the hardest of all trades, that of government". That old Greek philosopher made a lot of sense. I had no illusions that I would be an expert in this field and soon found out that it was quite different from my career in medicine where I felt everyone respected the decisions I made. In case anyone doesn't know, I would like to make it crystal clear that not all people think their Mayor is a great guy.

In this business a great many matters come before council where we have to make a judgement decision based upon the evidence and facts presented by people who may have very different and opposing ideas. We all know that one aspect of the same issue will prevail. Those who did not come out on the winning side can become quite upset and unreasonable at times regardless of whether it was a zoning application, a variance request, an objection over a new bylaw or a disagreement amongst neighbours that in hindsight didn't amount to a hill of beans.

Over the years I served with quite a number of elected officials on Comox Council and worked with mayors and councillors in other municipalities - both men and women. Not infrequently we may have had different views on a matter before us and I feel that this difference was a good thing because when the debate was over usually a consensus was reached and shared that was in the community's best interest. I also have strong feelings that the great majority had, as their main concern, the interest of their town or city at heart and were genuinely trying to do the right thing.

There is always some new problem to face in civic politics, some new crisis or some issue where opposing factions line up against each other or against council. But I feel quite good about the many decisions we made after reaching a consensus around the table. Sure we may have made some mistakes but I think they were quite minor in nature. And it is so easy to criticize from the sidelines. As I reflect back on some of the great debates and important directions we took, I have a deep sense of pride and thank the dozens of councillors who partcipated in the process over the years.

I guess one of the major decisions to be taken was joining with our neighbouring city, Courtenay, in our plan to solve our sewage disposal concerns. Prior to that Comox discharged raw sewage into the ocean and Courtenay was having problems with their failing sewage lagoon at the end of Comox Bay. Neither situation could continue in the interest of our environment. So in a joint effort we built a treatment plant for secondary treatment. It was a very costly undertaking but it had to be done.

I was pleased to see the acquisition of considerable blocks of land for future park development and proud of some of the development that occurred in this designated space. During my term we acquired the Filberg Home and 2 acres on the shore. I set up the Filberg Home and Park Association to administer this great asset and I played a major role in negotiating the purchase price and subsequent purchase of the remaining 9 acres at this site from the Vancouver Foundation.

I was also the Mayor when we extended our boundaries to include the land owned by the Department of Defence and which included the Military and Civilian Airport.

I am very proud of the new Community Centre which was another costly adventure but am happy to see it playing such a role for our citizens. I think only a few know that I actually drew and submitted the plans for this complex and, with just a few minor changes by the designer, it was accepted as the best concept. This was my only attempt at getting into another career - that of being an architect!

The list of projects and decisions made could go on and on. The debates and deliberations on many of these issues are now long forgotten. But the impact on this great town and the way of life of its citizens will continue, in my view, to be very significant. That, of course, will be for those citizens to decide and make up their own minds as to whether we acted responsibly and chose wisely. It all gives me a lot to reflect upon.

It is recorded in the records of the Municipal Affairs Department in Victoria that I was the Mayor who brought in the first official Community Plan for a municipality in B.C. These documents, although not written in stone and can be altered, set out a plan for the future of that town or city. The Comox Plan has been altered a few times but only after public hearing and input from the citizens. Sometimes they are not popular but I think our beautiful town would have developed in a very different way without it. It is now mandatory that every municipality in B.C. must have such a plan.

I soon learned that one had to be careful when discussing matters with the news media. On one memorable occasion the reporter's story caused National headlines. It occurred at the time of the crisis in Asia when many thousands were fleeing from Viet Nam and became known as the "boat people". A decision had been made in Ottawa that Canada would accept a quota of these poor souls. Apparently it had been decided that

Canadian Forces Base Comox would be the landing spot for the 747 jets that were going to transport them to Canada for dispersal, at a later date, to various parts of the country. Well, I was asked what the Mayor of Comox thought about these thousands of people arriving in our town. My reply was quite clear - I thought. I stated that if it had been decided that this was to be the arrival destination prior to placement, I was sure the personnel at the base would make them feel welcome. The headlines in the press read "The mayor of Comox welcomes the decision to settle the Viet Nam refugees in the Valley". I had not given my interview with the reporter another thought until the next day when the phone began ringing - calls from Comox residents and elsewhere that were very upset about my decision to accept this large influx of people to become residents of the area, and that is putting it mildly. We were in the midst of an unemployment period at the time and I was questioned as to what we were going to do to employ these numbers. Some even questioned my sanity. The Comox Valley did accept our share of these people in the final analysis. However it is so easy to be misquoted.

Every once in a while on Council, one comes face to face with a major issue. Such occurred over a ruling by the Department of National Defence dealing with a future subdivision in Comox that lay in one of the flight paths from the airport. At the end of every runway a strip of land extends for some distance from the runway. Also extending from the end of each runway is an imaginary line - a 2% sloping line where nothing can be built if the height of construction crosses this plane.

As was our policy to notify D.N.D. of any future

construction or subdivision in the proximity of the base, we sent them our plans for this development which was actually in the highest area of our town. We received a letter from them vetoing such a proposal because it violated the height restriction in this flight path.

We had invested a lot of planning time to this project and were taken by surprise and were quite upset because it was also known to us that this same department in far off Ottawa had sold, just a few years before, a fairly large parcel of land in the middle of this proposed development to our School Board for the purpose of building a school. This construction was completed and approved by D.N.D. and became the site of Highland Secondary School housing some 1500 students. The actual flight elevation line on this particular flight path ran 15 feet under the foundation of the school. I guess they didn't know that we had some fairly high hills in this area. In any event it was time for the gloves to come off. I guess there developed a quick need for some action. We even had the Chief of Defence Staff General Withers come out to Comox for a press conference where he produced a letter from Defence Minister Giles Lamontagne to me stating "It is our policy to zone all military airfields to provide protection - but in this particular instance the operational requirement for runway number 1836 does not require strict adherence to our criteria." It also states that a mistake had been made and that the approach surface slope would be raised from 2% to 5%.

I think this document should be preserved as an example of 1- passing the buck, 2- covering one's butt and 3- changing the rules in mid stream to solve a problem. Thankfully the crisis was over.

During my years as Mayor I was elected as a director of the Association of Vancouver Island Municipalities (A.V.I.M.). This is an association representing all of the municipalities on Vancouver Island and the Sunshine Coast. We have always had many concerns to discuss at our conventions as we acted as a single body to present those concerns to our senior governments. They mostly stemmed from the fact that although the Island had approximately 1/5 of the population of the Province and supplied a great deal of their general revenue because of our resource industries, namely forestry, we were not, in our view, getting our fair share of the benefits. Our goat trail up the Island, in spite of years of promises for a new highway, our shortage of electricity, our absence of natural gas, the ferry problems, were just a few of our concerns.

In 1980 I became the president of this association and had the task of putting together an agenda for our convention which was to be held in Courtenay that year. The theme for our deliberation was to deal with our energy problems. At that time we were having brown outs because of lack of electricity at peak usage times. We were also probably the last general area in Canada that did not have the availability of natural gas.

I was able to line up a pretty impressive array of speakers for the meeting including Dr. Gordon Shrum, the boss man of B.C. Hydro. I also had a president of Inland Natural Gas as well as others.

The big problem, of course, was getting these two power sources to the Island. Hydro was in the planning stage of bringing an underwater power line from the mainland to French Creek on the Island known as the Chekeye Dunsmuir proposal. Also receiving consideration was the building of an underwater gas line that would either come across near Victoria or alternately at Comox. There were many pros and cons to both these proposals and both were very costly undertakings.

During that year I began getting calls from a gentleman in Vancouver who proposed a solution to all our problems. His plan was to build a new highway and railroad from the interior to tidal water over the old route that was considered when they were going to build the C.P.R. line that eventually ended in Vancouver. This was known as the Waddington Trail Route and is well documented, as I found out when I went to the library to see what he was talking about. He then proposed building 3 short bridges, the last one being across Seymour Narrows at the site of the famous Ripple Rock, that was finally blown to bits, and arriving on the Island just north of Campbell River. On this route and over his bridges he would bring the new power and gas lines, a railway to have access to a deep sea port at Gold River on the West coast of the Island and it would also solve a great deal of the ferry problems as we would then have road access to the Island from the mainland. He was certainly persistant in his desire to present this proposal to us.

Well, I really didn't know any of this country where the route would exist and it all seemed a bit far fetched to me. So I got in touch with Alec Fraser, who at that time was Minister of Highways for B.C. He was a person who knew this part of the world very well and didn't mix words. He said he would speak to him but he stated to me that "the man is daft". I don't know what transpired but I never heard from this gentleman again nor have I heard the Waddington Route mentioned either.

Representing our association at meetings with the government in Victoria was always interesting and not always successful in our desire to get more for the Island, but we kept trying.

In Dec. 1990 I sought the Mayor's chair again for the last time and was successful. Soon afterwards I suddenly became ill which required a major operation. I had an aneurysm of my abdominal aorta that was in the process of rupturing. When I graduated from medicine, back in 1949, there was no cure, but thanks to the skills of a great surgical team and for vortex tubing that they used to replace the artery, I survived. I was sworn into office by a magistrate at the Royal Jubilee Hospital.

But changes were soon to be made. I gave up my medical practice to begin with. I had had a pretty good run at it and actually had limited my practice during the last year to just assisting at surgeries. So it was time to call it quits.

I was still Mayor but in the spring my physician suggested that it was probably time to think about giving up that part of my life as well. So I submitted my resignation in my first year of a three year term ending my years in civic politics - I thought. A couple of years later I got back at it but not as Mayor. I ran for councillor and spent the next 3 years at the Town Hall in that capacity, thus ending 19 years on council. Those years had passed so quickly and as I write this I realize that it represented exactly 1/4 of my life.

Two very interesting careers had finally come to an abrupt end. I was to start practicing up on becoming a retired, unemployed, senior citizen. But I had no concern about that stage in one's life and looked forward to it with equal enthusiasm and interest. I knew I would find much to do to keep me active.

INAUGURATION NIGHT

JANSON

'You just sit here, George, and we'll tell you when you've won.'

SWEARING IN AT ROYAL JUBILEE HOSPITAL - VICTORIA

THINGS THEY MAKE MAYORS DO

OPINION

FREE PRESS '91

First-class mayor deserves thanks

Comox, and the entire Valley around it, owe a debt of gratitude to outgoing mayor George Piercy, who retired from public life on Saturday after 16 years in local politics.

A stroke has slowed the former mayor to the point he can no longer handle the pressures of community leadership, but it cannot tarnish the long record of accomplishment he achieved during his years at the helm of the Town of Comox.

The town has grown tremendously during the Piercy era, and yet it has not lost the village-by-the-sea character that ranks it high among the most desirable places to live in Canada, and even the world. The community plan that Piercy helped develop, and defended diligently from the ravages of profiteering, has a great deal to do with the continuing liveability of Comox.

But the real magic of Piercy's administration has been his ability to maintain and expand these services without plunging the town into ruinous debt. Any politician can do great things today by mortgaging someone else's tomorrow, but Piercy always kept council away from that deadly mistake. Because of his ongoing patience, and his "do a bit at a time" and "pay as we go" philosophies, the Town of Comox is in a financial position that most communities can only dream about.

This newspaper has often taken issue with the decisions council made under the leadership of the outgoing mayor, but we have never doubted his good intentions, sincerity or dedication to the difficult task he faced for 16 years.

George Piercy, for a job well and truly done, to a standard that few can achieve or even aspire, we say thank you. May your well-deserved retirement be long and fruitful.

Good luck and God bless.

CHAPTER XIII

Reflections

When one tries to write a book on one's life, I don't think it is too uncommon for a person to wonder where it has all gone. As one recalls those years the highlights flash before you as if watching a moving screen unfold before you bringing to light so many events. There may have been some sad times but fortunately the happy times and memorable experiences stand out clearly. One may wonder why they did this or that and ask themselves the question of how they would deal with a particular matter if they had the chance to face that issue again.

It has given me the opportunity to reflect on my young years growing up and having the unique experience of living in a very rural semi-isolated community. Few have that experience in today's busy and crowded world.

As I think of isolated communities my thoughts drift back to when my great grandfather arrived here after giving up his established life in New Brunswick for a part of the world where few lived. I think of their journey by sailing ship up the coast and compare it to our time when travel by plane and ferry and the automobile is a way of life.

As I reflect on that heritage I am reminded of the profound effect their actions and decisions have had on my life today. We must never forget that and must maintain our respect for that great influence and that generation.

The spirit of sharing of what one had was certainly different than what we experience today. This early pioneer to our area with his wife, five sons and two daughters, of which the eldest son (my grandfather) was married with four children, stayed the first winter at Gartley Beach with a cousin whose arrival had preceded their long trek. As I total their numbers I am firmly convinced that if 14 of my relatives moved in with me, it would be a very long long winter.

I am extremely thankful that my youth was spent in a home with such caring and loving parents whose principles I hold dearly. They are both gone now - Dad in 1969 and my Mother in 1999 at the age of 97. We were so fortunate to have her around for so many years. The happy thoughts of them will always be with us. Gone as well is my brother, Jack and my only sister, Zeta. My youngest brother, Wes, still lives on Denman and we see each other often. But the memories of those years together as a family can never be erased.

As I write this Doris and I are planning to celebrate our 50th anniversary in just a few weeks, reminding me of the happy times we shared. And without her counsel on many issues, my life may not have unfolded as it did. In addition to our three children we have 9 grandchildren and 6 great grandchildren. They have started arriving in pairs now. My last two great grandchildren are identical twin girls. So we have certainly added a few names to Grandpa Matt Piercy's previous list of direct descendents. Watching this clan grow and develop adds a great deal of enjoyment to retired life.

Last year my graduating class met at McGill to celebrate the 50th anniversary of our graduation from medical school and 26 of the class of 155 were there. I'm sure their thoughts were like mine about the many changes that had occurred over that time and how very different medicine is at the present.

Today we often hear of some of the wonders of this change - the dramatic events in medicine such as organ transplants or open heart surgery and many others. These are dramatic and exciting procedures and are so important and were unheard of as we started out. All that we could do was to advise the patients to get their affairs in order as there was so little that we could do for so many of those illnesses.

But my thoughts go back over the years and I think of the less spectacular changes that we tend to forget about and yet have been responsible for greater benefits to humans. I think of the great advances in early diagnois that have saved so many lives - most noticeably the introduction of the pap test for early detection of cancer of the cervix and more recently the P.S.A. test for cancer of the prostate. There are the new diagnostic tools such as the C.A.T. scan or an M.R.I. that are now available. We saw the introduction of new vaccines such as the polio vaccine and the measle innoculations just to name a couple.

The countless new medicines including the antibiotics and the drugs for mental illness have made such a difference. Some diseases have been completely eliminated. This list of changes to our life styles and our health is endless and could be the subject for a different book.

So as one of that group of 50 years ago these changes have been unbelievable and thankfully have had such benefit to our lives. The grads of today, I'm sure, will see even greater advances in their lifetime. It will all be so challenging and interesting. I trust all of them approach their careers as eagerly and with the enthusiasm and dedication that our class did and it is my sincere hope that the practice of medicine will be as enjoyable as it has been to the class of '49. Only time will answer that.

My life as a family physician was the only way I wanted it and certainly have no regrets about not limiting my practice to one field of endeavor. Becoming involved with the care of a family and sharing with them the many facets of their life was an extremely satisfactory work. I read a recent article in the medical journal discussing the dwindling number of primary care or family physicians and I feel that this is an unfortunate development for the population in general.

I will only briefly comment on the state of our medicare system as one sees it today. It is changing rapidly.

I was fortunate to have spent most of my working years under the universal health care system that was second to none. I have been around long enough to have also practised at a time before medicare and know of some of the problems and hardships that patients experienced at that time. But I have watched the decline of this great system while I was still practising. Since then I have kept in touch with the medical body and know of their unhappiness and their concerns about the system today. The long waits for hospital beds and the increasing number of patients waiting to have a certain surgical procedure, the shortage of nursing staff, the lack of long term care facilities, the increased paper work and red tape that has added nothing to the quality of care, the great drain of our skilled and qualified physicians and surgeons who have left our country to practise elsewhere are all major concerns.

It saddens me to speak with my colleagues and hear of so much discontent. The really sad part is that the politicians quite often feel that all will be well again and offer some expedient, myopic and bandaid approach to solving the problem. Some major changes must be addressed if the system is going to survive. It is certainly my sincere hope that it will survive but it is going to take some meaningful dialogue between all of the parties - the politicians of both senior levels of government, the professionals in the delivery system of medicine and the users. All aspects must be considered to determine what type of coverage will be available in the future and finding out what we want from the health care system. Shifting blame from one level of government to the next re the financing is not going to solve any problems other than possibly for a short time. The issues are far greater than that and throwing more money at the system is not the answer.

My second career in civic politics has also been a rewarding challenge that I undertook and it leaves one with a sense of pride as I look back over those years. The town more than doubled in population during my tenure and as one may imagine the pressures for more growth were before me all the time. It could have developed in a very different way. Our concept of a "Village by the Sea" has endured and over the years I had countless letters from citizens and visitors alike who felt we had a very attractive town.

Comox received municipal status in 1947. Many many changes have taken place since that incorporation. Every once in a while I listen to some person who is disenchanted with any change in the community or the world, and who quite often is very vocal about their concerns. Quite often they express the opinion that it would be great to be like the "old days" in the town. Well I just have to bite my tongue because I guess I can count myself as one who lived here in the "old days" and I think of what we had in those days. The streets were gravelled roads and very dusty and without any street lighting or sidewalks. Beside the road we had open ditches that frequently smelled and let us know that a septic field was leaching into them. Our water was from wells and springs and had a sulphur smell and turned our utensils (and occasionally our teeth) black. We had few of the amenities that we enjoy in today's world. If this is what these malcontents want, I say "forget it" because here is one person who doesn't want to revert to that era. We will continue to have changes and I trust they will be for the benefit of the town as a whole.

My interests in politics were only at the municipal level and I am thankful that I did not accept the offers of political parties to run for elected office in senior government in spite of their polls and surveys telling them that I should do so. Getting elected may have been a different matter but I was just not the least bit interested in spite of their "wining and dining" efforts to get me to do so.

Of course my involvement with the A.V.I.M. made my political life very memorable. For my efforts there I was awarded a life membership in the association.

I am encouraged to see some younger men and women entering civic affairs in spite of Aristotle's statement that people who do that are untrained and unqualified. This business is something that has to be learned and experienced as one's term progresses. Using common sense, not bowing to the wishes of certain very vocal pressure groups, and looking sincerely at the broad picture of what is best for one's community is all that is needed. I trust that we will continue to see more and more of this younger generation come forth.

I have had many letters of appreciation from so many community organizations and citizens that I met and worked with over the years. I have also received quite a number of honors and awards for which I am appreciative. However these were not the reasons I became involved. People sometimes ask why I became involved with the different organizations and with civic politics. I do not have the answer as to what body chemistry motivated me to do these things. I was in the position where I could have retired quite some years before I did and settled into a life of relaxation but in my heart I know that I would not have been happy. I just wanted to offer my services to the town which is very special to me and I hope my efforts were appreciated.

I started out on this project to just write a short outline of my life so that my family would have a record of just who George Piercy was and what he did. I guess I got carried away but I trust they will read it with interest. If any others enjoy the book, that will be a bonus.

I am thankful to have had the life I did. There are great memories about so many events as my life unfolded. But the highlights centre around my family which has meant so much to me and the many, many great friends that I have met over the years in two very different careers.

As the young people say "It has been a slice".

WHO SAID RETIREMENT IS A TOUGH LIFE

WITH MY BROTHER WES
ON MOTHER'S 90TH BIRTHDAY

OCT 98

Rotary honors for Dr. Piercy

❑ Award recognizes community work of former mayor

The Comox Rotary Club honoured Dr. George Piercy with its 1998 Paul Harris Fellowship Award on Thursday, October 1.

After an introduction by club member Gwyne Mack, Assistant District Governor Doug Ante made the presentation of medallion, certificate and pin to Dr. Piercy.

Club president Paul Ives then presented Dr. Piercy's spouse, Doris, with flowers in recognition of her support for Dr. Piercy's community activities.

The Paul Harris Fellowship Award represents a contribution of $1,000 in U.S. funds to the Rotary International Foundation in the name of the recipient.

Dr. George Piercy, right, accompanied by his wife Doris, is honored with the Comox Rotary Club's annual Paul Harris Fellowship award, presented by Rotary Assistant District Governor Doug Ante

Association of Vancouver Island Municipalities

This will certify that

George Piercy

has been elected a

Life Member

of the

ASSOCIATION of VANCOUVER ISLAND MUNICIPALITIES

at the Annual Meeting of the Association

held in Courtenay, British Columbia *on*

March 10-12 19 95

This Life Membership was granted as an appreciation

of your years of service to local government and to AVIM and its Executive.

Maxine P. Williams
President

Lydia Fraser
Secretary

THE COMMEMORATIVE MEDAL FOR THE 125TH ANNIVERSARY OF THE CONFEDERATION OF CANADA IS CONFERRED UPON	**LA MÉDAILLE COMMÉMORATIVE DU 125È ANNIVERSAIRE DE LA CONFÉDÉRATION DU CANADA EST CONFÉRÉE À**

Dr. George Piercy

in recognition of significant contribution to compatriots, community and to Canada	*en reconnaissance de sa contribution significative au bien-être de ses compatriotes, sa communauté et au Canada*

1867 – 1992

Gouverneur général du Canada

Governor General of Canada

IN MY GARDEN PRETENDING TO BE A FARM BOY AGAIN